W9-AFB-813

Iran's Economic Morass

Mismanagement and Decline under the Islamic Republic

Eliyahu Kanovsky

Policy Paper No. 44

THE WASHINGTON INSTITUTE FOR NEAR EAST POLICY

© 1997 by the Washington Institute for Near East Policy

Published in 1997 in the United States of America by the Washington Institute for Near East Policy, 1828 L Street N.W. Suite 1050, Washington, DC 20036

Library of Congress Cataloging-in-Publication Data

Kanovsky, Eliyahu.
    Iran's economic morass: mismanagement and decline under the Islamic Republic/ Eliyahu Kanovsky.
        p. cm. —(Policy papers ; no. 44)
    ISBN 0-944029-67-1
    1. Iran—Economic policy. 2. Iran—Economic conditions—1979-
I. Title. II. Series: Policy Papers (Washington Institute for Near East Policy) ; no. 44
HC475.K363 1997   97-28107
338.955--dc20   CIP

Cover design by Debra Naylor.

The Author

Eliyahu Kanovsky is professor of economics and a senior research associate at the BESA Center for Strategic Studies at Bar Ilan University in Israel. He is also the Ludwig Jesselson Visiting Professor of Economics at Yeshiva University in New York.

Dr. Kanovsky is the author of numerous studies of the economics of the Middle East, including four previous Washington Institute Policy Papers: *Another Oil Shock in the 1990s? A Dissenting View* (1987), *OPEC Ascendant? Another Case of Crying Wolf* (1990), *The Economic Consequences of the Persian Gulf War: Accelerating OPEC's Demise* (1992), and *The Economy of Saudi Arabia: Troubled Present, Grim Future* (1994).

The opinions expressed in this Policy Paper are those of the author and should not be construed as representing those of the Washington Institute for Near East Policy, its Board of Trustees or Board of Advisors.

Contents

Acknowledgments

I have benefited greatly from the cooperation of the administration and staff of Yeshiva University. My respect and gratitude are extended to President Norman Lamm, Vice President Dr. Sheldon Socol, Academic Vice President Dr. William Schwartz, and Deans Norman Adler and Karen Bacon. Ceil Levinson of the Office of the Dean at Yeshiva College has at all times been very helpful. John Moryl of the Pollack Library has been very cooperative.

During the past few years I have been privileged to occupy the chair in economics at Yeshiva University, named after Ludwig Jesselson, of blessed memory. My respects and gratitude are extended to Erica Jesselson and her family.

Special thanks are due to the staff of the Department of Economics and the economics library at Bar Ilan University. I am especially indebted to Sylvia Sack in the Office of the Dean of Social Sciences for her patient typing of statistical tables.

At the Washington Institute for Near East Policy, my thanks to Dr. Robert Satloff, his colleagues, and staff—particularly editors *extraordinaire* John Wilner and Eden Bossom.

Crucial to this and other endeavors has been the encouragement and forbearance of my wife Tamar during our fifty years of marriage. If, while immersed in my studies, I paid less attention to her, our children, grandchildren, and great grandchild, I trust they will be forgiving. *Baruch Hashem.*

Eliyahu Kanovsky
March 1997

Executive Summary

In the latter half of the 1990s, the Iranian economy faces horrendous problems: economic mismanagement, high inflation, declining living standards, a growing gap (much of it fueled by pervasive corruption) between a wealthy minority and vast impoverished majority, high rates of unemployment, an inability to significantly increase oil production (concurrent with lower oil prices), stagnant *per capita* investment and GDP, serious problems in the manufacturing sector, and a heavy burden of foreign debt. As a result, the rate of annual economic growth in recent years (1993-96) has averaged 1.5 percent, well below the 3 percent annual growth in population.

In other words, *per capita* GDP has been declining since 1993, and projections for the remainder of the decade indicate a continuation of this trend. This implies deteriorating employment capacity and a further drop in living standards for the majority of Iranians; if, as anticipated, oil prices decline from the unusually high levels in 1996, Iran's economic troubles will be even worse.

Between 1977—the last year under the shah and relatively unaffected by revolutionary turmoil—and 1996, Iran's GDP declined by about one-third,[1] and on a *per capita* basis by a calamitous 50 percent. According to official estimates, average living standards (real private consumption *per capita*) dropped 20 percent. (Unofficial estimates of inflation—which are much higher—make the decline even more severe.) Moreover, these are economy-wide averages. In view of the increasing income gap and unequal income distribution, the poorest and middle income groups suffered an even greater decline than indicated by the national averages, while the wealthy elite have become richer.

Iranian officials continue to cast much of the blame for the current mess on the bloody and costly eight-year war with Iraq (1980-88). In addition to the tragedy of those killed and wounded, there was heavy economic damage. Iraq's bombing of oil installations, electric power plants, bridges, manufacturing plants, and other infrastructure required large expenditures for reconstruction. Not long after the 1988 ceasefire with Iraq, however, there was an increase in world oil prices in 1989, which was followed by a much stronger climb in oil prices in 1990-92 as a result of the 1991 Persian Gulf War and its aftermath. As a result, Iran received a "bonus" of about $10 billion in oil export revenues compared to 1980-82—even after adjusting for revenue from increases in the volume of its oil exports.

This indicates that the long-term impact of the Islamic revolution and subsequent mismanagement of the economy were at least as important as

---

[1] Economist Intelligence Unit, *Country Profile–Iran* (1996-97), p.14; *Country Report–Iran*, no. 4 (1996), pp. 5-12.

the war with Iraq in accounting for Iran's acute current economic problems. Perhaps of greatest importance was the mass flight during and following the revolution of an estimated two to four million entrepreneurs, professionals, technicians, and skilled craftspeople (and their capital) whose absence is felt to this day. The flight of their capital to safehavens abroad depressed investment within Iran, which in turn had negative long-term effects on growth, employment, income, and other economic factors.

Much of the property, factories, banks, and other enterprises abandoned by the shah, his family and entourage, and others who fled Iran was either nationalized by the Islamic Republic or given to newly created charitable foundations known as *bonyads*. Some of these *bonyads* have become major conglomerates operating in a wide variety of industries and services. They are solely under the control of religious leaders and benefit from various implicit and explicit subsidies.

Though most of Iran's generally small industrial enterprises are private, since the Islamic revolution industrial production has been dominated by the public sector. In many cases, the state-owned enterprises incur losses and must be subsidized by the public treasury. Various laws that prevent firing redundant workers tend to increase disguised unemployment and require heavier state subsidization.

Managers of public sector enterprises are often selected on the basis of their "Islamic correctness" rather than competence. This tolerance of poor management has been further institutionalized through the practice of reserving nearly half of the spaces for new students in the universities for those who are Islamically correct and exempting them from taking the standard entrance examinations. Lower academic standards ultimately result in a smaller pool of qualified professionals.

A system of multiple exchange rates introduced and later greatly expanded in the 1980s continues to distort the efficient allocation of resources by encouraging investment in trade and distribution rather than industry. In addition, it encourages importers and exporters to cheat the government out of scarce foreign exchange by over-invoicing imports or under-invoicing exports, often with the collusion of corrupt officials. A more recent version (introduced in 1995) created two official exchange rates: 1,750 rials and 3,000 rials to the dollar, compared to a black market rate that fluctuated in the latter months of 1995 in the range of 3,500 to 4,500 rials to the dollar. Regulations require non-oil exporters, largely from the private sector, to sell all foreign currency to the central bank at the rate of 3,000 rials to the dollar. This encourages corruption, resort to the free (black) market, and hiding foreign currency earnings abroad. Though the Islamic government has for many years tried to reduce Iran's overwhelming dependence on oil exports by promoting exports by other sectors of the economy, these exchange rate mechanisms tend to achieve precisely the opposite effect.

The International Monetary Fund, World Bank, and many Iranian economists have encouraged the government to adopt a single, market-oriented exchange rate, but opposition to such a change is powerful. Businessmen with access to the government ministries—often through corruption—are able to obtain import permits that guarantee importers a very large and automatic profit and amount to, in the words of one analyst, "a license to print money." Public officials who share in the spoils join the opposition to economic reforms.

Similarly, rather than liberalizing state controls to encourage production and enterprise, the government greatly expanded the list of price-controlled products in 1995. Though hardly unique to Iran, subsidies of such magnitude have few parallels elsewhere. Iran's budget includes explicit subsidies for basic foods, medicines, and other essential goods. But the implicit subsidies, which do not appear in the budget, are far greater. Essential goods are imported at the lower of the two exchange rates (i.e., 1,750 rather than 3,000 rials to the dollar). The most costly subsidy by far is the very low domestic price for gasoline and other oil products. Even the major oil exporting sheikhdoms of the Persian Gulf, with much smaller populations than Iran, do not charge such low prices. The result is that Iran's oil consumption has been rising very rapidly, in effect reducing the volume available for export. According to recent calculations, the annual cost of both explicit and implicit subsidies is about $15 billion—roughly equivalent to the country's total 1995 annual oil revenues.

In addition to businessmen and public officials, it appears that many Muslim clerics have succumbed to the lure of high living and corruption. In short, the opponents of basic reforms constitute a very powerful and thus far winning combination. Moreover, drastic reforms such as reducing or completely eliminating most subsidies would be painful to many poor and middle class Iranians in the short term by increasing inflationary pressures. A single market-oriented exchange rate, which would improve the balance of payments, would also raise domestic prices. Similarly, large-scale privatization would initially result in dismissals of unneeded workers who were kept on the payroll by public sector enterprises at the expense of the public treasury. In the long run, however, a more efficient market economy would emerge in which private firms seeking to take advantage of higher prices would absorb displaced workers and increase production, and—given appropriate fiscal and monetary policies—the forces of supply and demand would eventually raise output and lower prices.

During the war with Iraq, Khomeini's ideological bias against external borrowing was so strong that the revolutionary government actually reduced the foreign debt it had inherited from the shah. When Rafsanjani took over as president in 1989, however, he favored borrowing as a means to speed post-war reconstruction and development. Although Iran's oil export revenues rose sharply as a result of the higher oil prices accompanying the Persian Gulf War, imports rose even more rapidly and led to large deficits in the balance of payments. These deficits were financed, directly and indirectly, by external short-term credits.

In 1992, Iran was for the first time unable to pay its foreign obligations. After many meetings with its major European lenders and Japan, Tehran rescheduled its debt—lowering current payments by extending the payment period to five or six years. Thus, until the end of the decade, Iran faces the difficult task of financing current imports of the machinery and equipment, raw materials, and spare parts it desperately needs for investment and production, while simultaneously paying for imports of food and other essential goods and earning sufficient foreign exchange to repay its debts.

Since 1991, there have been bloody riots in various cities protesting inflation, unemployment, and deprivation. Though the government has employed harsh measures (including flogging and execution) against the rioters, the fear of an even more violent reaction deters it from undertaking the major reforms needed to jump-start the economy. Meanwhile, the present regime does not appear to have the political will to implement the far-reaching economic reforms needed to change course. Resistance to change and the political costs of economic reforms have both grown enormously.

Tehran may be hoping that some exogenous factor will lead to a sharp hike in the price of oil, providing another multi-billion dollar windfall to help it continue to muddle through. If a disruption (war, revolution, etc.) drastically reduced oil production in one or more of the large oil-exporting countries in the Middle East or elsewhere, oil prices would rise to the temporary benefit of other oil exporters. (Indeed, this phenomenon provided a short-term boost to Iranian oil revenues in 1996.) But the long-term trend is for lower oil prices, at least when measured in constant (inflation-adjusted) dollars. Despite the two major oil shocks in the 1970s, real oil prices today are near the 1973-74 level.

Although the 1990 Iraqi invasion of Kuwait and subsequent Persian Gulf War resulted in a major increase in oil prices, by 1993 oil prices were lower than before the war—even when measured in current dollars and with Iraqi exports tightly controlled due to continued sanctions against Iraq. The additional easing or eventual end of these sanctions will only further depress the price of oil and with it the economic problems Iran and other major oil exporting countries face.

The difficult economic situation has been exacerbated by the U.S. economic embargo. Although the failure of other industrialized countries to participate has limited the impact of the U.S. embargo, it has not been entirely ineffective. Indeed, by undermining business confidence, the sanctions make it even less likely that potential investors would consider investment in Iran in the face of U.S. hostility. The net result has rendered many of Iran's military ambitions unaffordable. Since 1992 or 1993 Iran has apparently curtailed its arms purchases and reportedly canceled some orders for military equipment. Further deterioration in the Iranian economy could lead to radical political change, which would have important ramifications both in the Middle East and globally.

Preface

Eighteen years ago, the Islamic Revolution in Iran sent shockwaves throughout the world. Espousing a radical version of Islam, Ayatollah Khomeini took power in one of the world's most strategically important locations. Shortly thereafter, his clerical regime orchestrated the seizure of the U.S. embassy and its staff in Tehran and dedicated itself to "exporting the revolution" to Muslim capitals from North Africa to the Gulf and beyond.

Today, nearly a decade after Khomeini's death, much of the Iranian revolution's initial vitality has dissipated. The horrendous human and material losses incurred during the eight-year war with Iraq were compounded by ideological and political infighting among factions vying for control of Khomeini's legacy, which has resulted in a combination of inconsistent policies and gross mismanagement that have wrecked Iran's post-war economy. With reactionary Majlis Speaker Ali Akbar Nateq Nuri heavily favored to succeed Hashemi Rafsanjani as president in elections scheduled for May 1997, the prospect for moderation in Iran's domestic, economic, or foreign policies appears dim.

Thus, while hobbled by a stagnant economy and U.S. sanctions, Tehran seems determined to continue its relentless drive to acquire an offensive naval capability in the Persian Gulf, ballistic missiles capable of striking U.S. allies and interests throughout the region, and—most menacing of all—weapons of mass destruction. And though only marginally successful in creating clone regimes throughout the Islamic world, Tehran shows little inclination to desist from leading a self-declared political, military, and cultural struggle against the West. From its earliest days in power, the clerical regime has been providing financial, logistical, and even operational support to terrorist groups such as Hamas, Hezbollah, and Islamic Jihad which seek to destabilize moderate U.S. allies from Bosnia to Bahrain, to scuttle the Arab-Israeli peace process, and ultimately to "liberate" historical Palestine.

In recent years, voices from across the American political spectrum have highlighted the threat that Iran poses to U.S. interests and the consequent need to take bold action to address Iran's rogue behavior. Targeting Iran's economy has been a key focus of these efforts, which have ranged from a trade embargo against Iran to the 1996 Iran and Libya Sanctions Act imposing punitive measures against third-country companies' investment in Iran's oil sector. Early signs suggest these efforts are bearing results, which Washington hopes will add impetus to the re-evaluation by some Europeans of their own strategy of "critical dialogue" with the clerical regime.

Given the systemic nature of the Iranian threat—arising not from a single personality (as in Iraq) but from a comprehensive worldview propagated by a state—it is of paramount importance to understand all aspects of Iranian strategy, politics, and economics. In that context, The Washington Institute is pleased to publish the last of three related research studies that comprise its "Focus on Iran" series. Written by world-renowned scholars from around the world, these monographs present timely information and expert analysis on the issues that matter most to U.S. regional interests—the nature of the Iranian military threat, the likely winners in the factional battles for political power in Tehran, and the strengths and vulnerabilities of the Iranian economy. Together, these Policy Papers constitute a comprehensive briefing for policymakers, journalists, diplomats, and others concerned about the "worst-case scenario" facing the United States and its allies at the end of the twentieth century—a nuclear-armed Islamic Republic of Iran.

In this final study in the series, distinguished Middle East economist Eliyahu Kanovsky presents a definitive assessment of the Iranian economy. Through detailed analysis of pre- and post-revolution economic data, Kanovsky examines Iran's largely unsuccessful efforts to diversify and privatize its mostly state-controlled economy—based almost exclusively on oil export revenues—in the midst of a long-term trend of declining world oil prices. *Iran's Economic Morass* chronicles how revolutionary ideology and political infighting have hampered the development of coherent economic policies, and how the resulting corruption, inflation, unemployment, and growing inequality between rich and poor have already sparked violent riots in several Iranian cities. Barring an unlikely increase in long-term oil prices, Kanovsky warns, the clerical regime appears incapable of undertaking the fundamental reforms that are necessary to prevent further deterioration. This, in turn, could lead to an even more radical Iran, as the *mullahs* seek to turn the attention of the Iranian masses away from domestic economic troubles and toward a common external adversary.

As the United States confronts the dangers that Iran and its acolytes pose throughout the world, we hope that the "Focus on Iran" series will increase awareness of the challenges that lie ahead.

Michael Stein	Barbi Weinberg
President	Chairman

I

Introduction

In mid-1993, *New York Times* correspondent Chris Hedges presented a very pessimistic assessment of Iran's economy:

> Fourteen years after the overthrow of the shah, the Iranian revolution has failed to achieve either prosperity or sustained hope. A costly eight-year war with Iraq, economic mismanagement, and endemic corruption, coupled with executions and arrests, have left the clerics who rule Iran isolated and ever more dependent on the repressive organs of state security for control. Discontent is widespread. . . . The end of the war [with Iraq] in 1988 was supposed to bring not only peace but prosperity. But Iranians who sacrificed their youth and careers and lost friends or kinsmen have been rewarded with mounting unemployment, high inflation, housing shortages, and a state-run economy that has driven industry to the ground.[1]

In a book published that year, Iranian scholar Jahangir Amuzegar came to similar conclusions:

> The Iranian economy's overall performance since the revolution has largely failed the test of both equity and efficiency. Continued heavy reliance on oil as the mainstay of the economy reveals that there has been no real progress toward economic diversification. . . . [P]er capita income has declined, the infrastructure has deteriorated, labor productivity has fallen, shortages have been intensified, and unsavory practices have spread far and wide.[2]

Another study, focusing on Iran's national security, concluded that

> The success of the revolution and the future of the Islamic Republic of Iran will be determined by its economic performance. The revolution today is a hollow shell that neither inspires nor animates its proponents. The costs of the war, economic mismanagement, corruption, rapid population growth, and the slide in the [price] of oil have combined to devastate the Iranian economy. By every indication, Iran is worse off economically than in the shah's reign. . . . Unless Iran improves its economic performance, it will face the prospect of civil disturbance. . . . Increasingly, it may have to rely on coercion to secure domestic order.[3]

---

[1] *New York Times (NYT)*, June 27, 1993, p. 2E.

[2] Jahangir Amuzegar, *Iran's Economy under the Islamic Republic* (London: I.B. Taurus & Co., 1993), p. 292.

[3] Shahram Chubin, *Iran's National Security Policy* (Washington, DC: Carnegie Endowment for International Peace, 1994), p. 78.

Following the ceasefire in 1988 and the election of Ali Akbar Hashemi Rafsanjani as president in 1989, there were optimistic assessments of Iran's economic future. Iraq's invasion of Kuwait and the subsequent U.S.-led campaign to oust Iraqi forces were an indirect blessing for Iran's economy because the fear of shortages raised oil prices. The near-total embargo of Iraqi oil exports (and of Kuwaiti exports while they were under Iraqi control) allowed other oil exporters, including Iran, to expand sales. Iran's oil export revenues rose sharply from $9.7 billion in 1988 to $16.9 billion in 1992. This in turn permitted a very large expansion of imports including machinery, spare parts, and raw materials, the lack of which had severely hampered industry and other economic sectors.[4]

In 1991, both the governor of the Central Bank and the finance minister extolled the favorable change in the economy as a result of liberalized import controls. They also noted that the system of multiple exchange rates, which had caused severe economic distortions, had been narrowed from twelve to three official exchange rates since January 1991. Moreover, they asserted that a uniform exchange rate would be implemented in the near future.[5] Interestingly, the American consulting firm DRI McGraw–Hill offered a rosy projection: "Given Iran's diverse natural resources, commercially strategic location, and highly motivated manpower, it has a good chance of becoming the leading Middle Eastern economy . . . by the turn of the century." [6]

The evidence available in 1996 did not support such optimistic assessments and projections—quite the contrary. A more detailed analysis, both micro and macro, of the Iranian economy should give us some insights as to Iran's economic future. Though the focus of this study is economic, the success or failure of the economy will have an important and possibly decisive impact not only on Iran's internal political stability but, indirectly, on the Middle East as a whole.

A NOTE ON IRANIAN STATISTICS

The Iranian national accounts are based on fiscal years beginning March 21. Thus, for example, fiscal year 1980 means March 21, 1980 through March 20, 1981. Unless otherwise stated in the text, 1980 refers to the fiscal year beginning March 21, 1980. Similarly, in the tables in the appendices, 1359/1980 refers to the year beginning March 21, 1980.

Like many other less developed countries, Iran's statistics are often incomplete and sometimes inaccurate. The estimates of inflation are based on prices fixed by the government, which are often subject to rationing. The index does not take into account the much higher price of goods in

---

[4] See Table 5.

[5] *Middle East Economic Digest (MEED)*, November 15, 1991, pp. 4-5.

[6] DRI/McGraw-Hill, *World Markets Report–Iran* (November 1994).

the flourishing black or free market. At times, rationed goods are simply not available and the black or free market becomes the only source.

Another major problem with Iranian statistics, particularly since the 1980s, has been the system of multiple exchange rates. In the early 1990s official exchange rates ranged from 70 to nearly 1,400 rials to the dollar. This extremely wide gap led to severe distortions and corruption. As is common in many less developed countries, military expenditures are camouflaged and deliberately understated.

In a 1984 Iranian Central Bank report, an unusually candid footnote observed that, "Considering the war-related expenditures and the dual pricing system in the economy [i.e., for goods that are price controlled and rationed, and are therefore purchased in substantial quantities in the free market], it is advisable that the results of national accounting, especially when it comes to the measurement of economic development and social welfare, be analyzed with caution."[7] The Central Bank report clearly implies that official price indices understate the real rate of inflation and thereby overstate the real rate of economic growth or understate the real rate of decline. Underestimating inflation also implies that real private consumption has risen less or fallen more than official figures would indicate. The statistical distortions of the 1980s apparently continue in the 1990s. Official estimates of inflation (the rise in the consumer price index) in 1994 were 31.5 percent;[8] unofficial estimates ranged from 50 to 100 percent.[9] Amuzegar states that the consensus among foreign analysts is that the Central Bank's price indices understate the true level of inflation "for both technical and political reasons."[10] Unless otherwise stated, the figures used are from official sources. Detailed data are given in the tables in the appendices.

---

[7] Central Bank of the Islamic Republic of Iran, *Economic Report and Balance Sheet* (1362), March 21, 1983 to March 20, 1984 , p. 17.

[8] See Table 3.

[9] *NYT*, May 20,1995, pp. A1, A8.

[10] Amuzegar, p. 70.

II

Iran's Economy: A Historical Overview

During the 1960s, the Iranian economy grew rapidly, with annual growth averaging 8.7 percent and rising to 10.6 percent between 1970 and 1977. The engine of this growth was a massive increase in oil export revenues from $700 million in 1960 to $2.1 billion in 1970 and $5.5 billion in 1973, and then skyrocketing to $23.6 billion in 1977. This windfall resulted primarily from far higher oil prices associated with the 1973-74 oil crisis,[1] and in turn financed investment in large-scale public infrastructure projects such as electric power, water systems, roads, air and sea ports, and communications, as well as modern industry and agriculture, health and educational facilities, and substantial improvements in Iran's military.

From 1970 to 1977, investment (gross fixed capital formation) rose by an annual average rate of 21 percent (measured in constant prices), with the private sector growth rate exceeding that of the public sector. Employment and income rose appreciably, and living standards (measured by real annual private consumption *per capita*) did so as well, by a very rapid 10.7 percent. Annual manufacturing production rose by 15.7 percent, and annual agricultural production expanded by a far more modest 4.6 percent. Non-oil gross domestic product (GDP) expanded at a very rapid pace of 12.6 percent annually, exceeding the growth rate of total GDP.[2] In the last two years of that span, investment averaged over 30 percent of GDP, about half of which came from the private sector (much of it in housing). By international standards, 30 percent of GDP constitutes a high rate of investment and usually presages high levels of economic growth.

The boom not only wiped out most unemployment, but also created labor shortages, which in turn induced an influx of foreign workers, particularly manual laborers from Afghanistan. The boom also induced the return of many Iranians who had earlier migrated to neighboring Arab countries in search of jobs. In fact, oil revenues grew so quickly that Iran was able to massively increase imports of goods and services from $3.1 billion in 1970 to $25.6 billion in 1977 while simultaneously increasing foreign exchange reserves from $1 billion in 1973 to $10.8 billion in 1977.[3]

---

[1] The oil crisis was caused by an Arab embargo in reaction to U.S. support for Israel during the October 1973 War.

[2] See appendices. Although the growth rate of non-oil GDP was impressive, the engine driving the non-oil sectors was the massive growth in government spending, which in turn was fueled by the flood of oil revenues accruing to the Iranian treasury.

[3] Tax revenues—primarily import duties—rose from 5 percent of GDP in 1974 to 9 percent

THE 1979 ISLAMIC REVOLUTION

Despite the unprecedented prosperity, there was growing opposition to the shah, and it was becoming more violent. Though most Iranians were better off, the gap between rich and poor was widening, due in part to corruption. Rapid economic growth increased inflationary pressures—in 1977 alone, the cost of living rose 27.6 percent, more than double the rate of the previous four years.[4] In most respects, 1977 was the peak year for the Iranian economy. As revolution-related turmoil grew in 1978, all major economic sectors (except agriculture) suffered declines. By December 1978, for example, crippling strikes initiated by Ayatollah Khomeini from exile in France brought Iran's oil exports to a halt. Overall, oil production declined almost 25 percent in 1978, with oil revenues dropping from $23.6 billion in 1977 to $17.1 billion. The political turmoil affected other sectors as well, including industry and construction. Only agriculture showed a modest gain, because rioting and other disruptions were largely confined to urban areas. As a whole, Iran's GDP fell 21.1 percent in 1978, while non-oil GDP fell a more modest 7.1 percent.

In February 1979, Khomeini returned to Iran and assumed the reins of power. This precipitated a mass exodus of professionals, managers, technicians, entrepreneurs, and other skilled workers needed to maintain a thriving economy, as well as large-scale capital flight, both of which continued into the 1980s. Although there are no official estimates, one study claimed that roughly two million Iranians "who possessed the skills necessary for running what was becoming an economically sophisticated state" left the country and that "[t]he mark of this loss is still instantly apparent in present-day Iran."[5] The *Economist* suggested that 3 million Iranians fled, but stressed their quality more than their absolute numbers, noting that they constitute "a huge reservoir of talent."[6] Still another estimate put the number of Iranians abroad at nearly four million and the flight of capital as high as $180 billion.[7] As one scholar noted,

> The revolutionary upheaval . . . led to a massive hemorrhage of capital. . . . However, the depletion of *human* capital was even more dramatic. . . . Iran, once regarded as one of the few Middle Eastern countries . . . with a fairly educated population, suddenly found itself not only short of capital, but of skilled labor.[8]

---

in 1978.

[4] See Table 3.

[5] Robert E. Looney, *Manpower Policies and Development in the Persian Gulf Region* (New York: Praeger, 1994), p. 66.

[6] *Economist,* May 2, 1992, p. 51.

[7] *Middle East Economic Digest (MEED)*, January 13, 1995, p. 5. Other estimates of capital flight range from $80-120 billion, but even these lower figures are greater than Iran's total oil revenues for 1989-93.

[8] M. Malek, "The Impact of Iran's Islamic Revolution on Health Personnel Policy," *World Development* 19, no. 8 (August 1991), pp. 1045-54 (emphasis added).

The clerical regime's economic policies favored reduced dependence on oil revenues, self-sufficiency in food supplies, and a sharp reduction in military expenditures (to be achieved by creating a citizens' army).[9] It abandoned many projects initiated by the shah. At the same time, the new constitution of the Islamic Republic specified that the public sector was to include "all major industries, foreign trade, major mines, banking, insurance, power, dams, major irrigation systems, air, sea, and land transport."[10] The new regime nationalized the banks, insurance companies, and larger firms, and imposed strict controls on what remained of the private sector. By 1982, the state-owned National Industrial Organization encompassed roughly 600 enterprises employing 150,000 people. The managers of the greatly expanded public sector were generally "loyal ideological supporters" of the regime chosen "irrespective of their ability to manage,"[11] and the adverse consequences of poor management were not long in coming.[12] The wholesale nationalization of industry after the revolution, coupled with the flight of both capital and human resources, left Iran's "still developing industrial base crippled."[13]

One of the more interesting phenomena was the establishment of *bonyads*—semi-public foundations run by clerics—to which the government gave the assets of the shah, his ruling elite, and other Iranians who fled the country after the revolution. These include hundreds of companies in all sectors of the economy. The *bonyads* are supposed to use profits from these enterprises to provide inexpensive housing, healthcare, and other social services to the poor.[14] In reality, much of it is siphoned off by those in control and relatively little reaches the needy. Though the *bonyads'* 1992-93 budget was equivalent to nearly half of the government's budget that year, the latter exercises very little control over these foundations, which answer only to the supreme leader.[15] According to one report, the Foundation for the Deprived and War Disabled became the largest and most powerful single economic institution in the country,

---

[9] Shahram Chubin and Charles Tripp, *Iran and Iraq at War* (Boulder, CO: Westview Press, 1980), p. 123.

[10] Alan Richards and John Waterbury, *A Political Economy of the Middle East* (Boulder, CO: Westview Press, 1990), p. 208.

[11] Ibid., p. 207.

[12] Hooshang Amirahmadi, *Revolution and Economic Transition: The Iranian Experience* (Albany, NY: State University of New York Press, 1990), p. 281.

[13] Economist Intelligence Unit (EIU), *Country Profile–Iran* (1994-95), p. 31.

[14] The largest of the *bonyads*, the Foundation for the Oppressed, reportedly made $400 million in profits in 1992; see *Economist*, September 25, 1993, p. 58.

[15] Hossein Askari, "It's Time to Make Peace with Iran," *Harvard Business Review* (January-February 1994), pp. 50-63. Iran's post-revolution constitution vested paramount religious and political authority in the supreme leader (*rahbar*); see David Menashri, *Revolution at a Crossroads: Iran's Domestic Politics and Regional Ambitions*, Policy Paper no. 43 (Washington, DC: Washington Institute for Near East Policy, 1997), p. 7.

employing some 350,000 workers.[16] According to a report in the *Economist,*

> the *bonyads* control a large portion of the economy. But with no shareholders, no public accounts, and answerable only to Iran's religious leader, the *bonyads* are a law unto themselves . . . . Attempts [by former owners] to reclaim confiscated property given to the *bonyads* after the revolution run into great obstacles.[17]

The economic policies of the new regime, coupled with the pre- and post-revolution turmoil, led to a recession. Between 1977 and 1980, GDP (in constant prices) declined by a massive 38.8 percent (46 percent *per capita*). Labor productivity deteriorated badly[18] and public sector enterprises (which dominate large-scale manufacturing) were operating at only a fraction of their capacities and incurring losses that required government subsidies to keep them solvent. Construction declined 19 percent, as evidenced by hundreds or thousands of abandoned construction sites. Official estimates show a small rise in the unemployment rate from 10.5 percent to 11.7 percent in 1980. Unofficial reports, however, paint a much darker picture: 25 percent of the labor force unemployed, despite government orders to both public and private enterprises to retain as many workers as possible, whether they were needed or not.[19] Living standards (measured by real private consumption *per capita*) fell by 22.2 percent.[20]

Though non-oil GDP fell by "only" 7.6 percent (16 percent *per capita*), the oil sector fell by a severe 83.3 percent. From April to June 1979, oil production averaged 3.9 million barrels per day (MBD), compared to 5.7 MBD in 1977 and the first nine months of 1978 (after which strikes began to reduce output). But the clerical regime was unable to maintain even this lower level of production, due apparently to the loss of many technical and managerial personnel from migration, arrest, and political dismissals. Production dropped to a mere 1.4 MBD in mid-1979. Oil exports,[21] which had ceased in December 1978, resumed under the new regime in the spring of 1979 but dropped precipitously from 5 MBD in 1977 and the first nine months of 1978 to less than 1 MBD in mid-1980.[22] The declining trend in oil production continued until the fall of 1980, reducing 1980 oil revenues to $11.7 billion, less than half of the $24 billion in 1976 and 1977.

---

[16] Jahangir Amuzegar, *Iran's Economy Under the Islamic Republic* (London and New York: I.B. Taurus & Co., 1993), p. 100.

[17] *Economist,* September 25, 1993, p. 58; see also *New York Times* (*NYT*), June 27, 1993, p. E2.

[18] This is evident from official statistics, which indicate that between 1977 and 1980, production by large manufacturing enterprises (those with ten or more workers) declined by 8 percent even as employment *rose* by 13 percent. See Table 9.

[19] *Financial Times* (*FT*), August 15, 1979, p. 10. Politically, the Islamic government preferred a large increase in hidden unemployment to further growth in overt unemployment.

[20] See appendices.

[21] Exports are derived from production minus domestic consumption.

[22] *Petroleum Economist,* various issues.

In response, the Iranian authorities drastically curtailed imports of goods and services from $25.6 billion in 1977 to $16.5 billion in 1980. This resulted in shortages of raw materials and spare parts for industry and other economic sectors. According to estimates by the U.S. Arms Control and Disarmament Agency (ACDA), Tehran also sharply reduced arms imports from a peak of $2.6 billion in 1977 to $420 million in 1980.[23] Despite these stringent curbs, Iran experienced a $2.4 billion balance of payments (current account) deficit in 1980 that contrasted sharply with its annual surpluses since 1973. Similarly, Iran's foreign exchange reserves fell from an all-time high of $14.6 billion in 1979 to $9.6 billion in 1980.

THE IRAN-IRAQ WAR, 1980-88

The September 1980 Iraqi invasion thus occurred at a time of rapid economic deterioration. Though the attack clearly did not initiate Iran's economic problems—the revolution had already inflicted severe blows on the economy (especially the oil sector) in the years before the war—the lengthy and costly war made a bad situation worse, causing serious economic damage for the first few years (though less than might have been expected). Desperate to revive the economy and finance the war effort, the authorities put the highest priority on increasing oil production and increasing export revenues.

Ironically, the cause of Iran's economic woes—the Islamic revolution—was also its salvation. The cessation of Iranian oil exports from late 1978 to early 1979, and concerns that the revolution could engulf the whole region triggered a second international oil crisis, in which prices skyrocketed from about $12 per barrel in 1978 to $35-40 in 1979-80. Though Iran's 1979 oil production was roughly 40 percent lower than in 1977, the higher prices kept oil export revenues about the same. Thus, when Iran's oil production rose from the paltry rate of 1.5 MBD in 1980-81 to an annual average of 2.6 MBD in 1980-85, annual oil export revenues climbed from $11.6 billion to $20.7 billion in 1982 and 1983. This (relative) bonanza in foreign exchange earnings permitted the authorities to increase imports, eliminating or greatly reducing the shortages of raw materials, spare parts, machinery, and equipment that had hampered industry and other economic sectors. Between 1980 and 1985, overall GDP advanced by an annual average rate of 5 percent, non-oil GDP rose more rapidly,[24] and investment (particularly private investment in housing) and living standards rose moderately.

In 1984, however, Iraq began to focus on economic targets, particularly Iran's oil installations and refineries, power plants, petrochemical facilities,

---

[23] See Tables 2 and 5. Arms imports are apparently excluded, in whole or in part, from the published balance of payments accounts; see EIU, *Country Profile–Iran* (1989-90), pp.42-44.
[24] See Tables 5 and 9.

and other industries, as well as tankers carrying Iranian crude oil to buyers. A Western correspondent noted with admiration that Iranian technicians "perform[ed] miracles" in quickly repairing damaged oil facilities.[25] Despite their heroic efforts, Iranian oil production fell from a wartime peak of 2.7 MBD in 1983 to 2.2 MBD in 1986.[26] Far more serious was the gradual erosion—and eventual collapse (in 1986)—of world oil prices. Iran's oil export revenues fell from $21.2 billion in 1983 to $13.7 billion in 1985, and then suffered a disastrous decline to $6.3 billion in 1986.[27] But even these figures understate the magnitude of Iran's financial calamity. As the so-called "tanker war" heated up in the Persian Gulf, insurance rates for ships in the war zone rose to the equivalent of $2.30 per barrel, a cost Tehran had to bear in order to induce foreign buyers to pick up its oil.[28] Moreover, heavy damage to its oil refineries compelled Iran to actually *import* nearly half of its refined petroleum products. Gasoline was rationed and there were shortages of heating oil.[29]

Iranian oil production recovered somewhat in 1987-88, averaging 2.5 MBD annually as compared to 2.2 MBD in 1986. World oil prices rose in 1987, but fell again in 1988. Iran's oil export revenues rose from the disastrously low $6.3 billion in 1986 to $10-11 billion in 1987-88, but were still far below the $21.2 billion earned in 1983. Despite the rapid expansion of its domestic military industries, Iran was compelled to use scarce foreign exchange to import sophisticated arms in order to counter Iraq's acquisition of advanced weapons from the Soviet Union, France, and others. According to ACDA estimates, annual Iranian arms imports rose from an average of $1.1 billion during 1981-83 to $2.3 billion in 1984-88.[30]

With the exception of factories producing munitions, industry was operating at 30 percent of capacity. Annual imports of raw materials, spare parts, and machinery for civilian uses were sharply curtailed from a post-revolutionary peak of $18 billion in 1983 to about $11 billion in 1986-88. Severe shortages hampered industry and other economic sectors. Other than basic necessities, many consumer goods were in short supply. Moreover, chronic power outages adversely affected both industry and households.[31] In the last three years of the war (1985-88), Iran's GDP declined 21 percent (or about 28 percent *per capita*). Non-oil GDP also fell in the latter half of the 1980s, though not nearly as steeply. Manufacturing dropped by about one-third, and construction also fell sharply. Of the major economic sectors, only agriculture showed any gains. According to official statistics (which underestimate inflation), living standards declined

---

[25] *MEED*, December 13, 1986, p. 43.

[26] See Table 4.

[27] See Table 5.

[28] *Gulf States Newsletter*, January 11, 1988, pp. 8-11.

[29] *MidEast Markets*, February 22, 1988, p. 6.

[30] See Tables 2 and 5.

[31] EIU, *Country Profile–Iran* (1988-89), p. 34; *Middle East* (November 1988), pp. 23-24.

27 percent in the same period. Inflation was rampant, and investment was down a disastrous 47 percent.[32] Despite large-scale civilian mobilization and overstaffing in industry, the civil service, and other sectors, unemployment reached a dangerous 28.6 percent in 1986.[33]

THE 1988 CEASEFIRE

Ayatollah Khomeini conditioned acceptance of a July 1987 UN ceasefire resolution on several concessions, including massive reparations from Iraq and the removal of Saddam Hussein. In June 1988, the *Economist* reported from Tehran that "[s]even years of warfare have . . . brought destitution to Iran's economy. Iranians are growing tired of making sacrifices for a conflict which seems unwinnable. The supply of martyrs is drying up."[34] At about the same time, a *New York Times* report concluded that "the ability of the Iranian economy to stand up to the combined pressures of war and lower oil prices . . . is beginning to crumble."[35]

Other foreign observers, however, downplayed Iran's economic problems and their possible impact on its ability to continue the war. One journalist reported in early 1988 that living standards in Iran had "declined dramatically"—particularly among middle class office workers, civil servants, and teachers—but concluded that "the Islamic Revolution does not . . . face collapse. Far from it; it has weathered the drop in oil prices and the hostility of the West. The country is well-administered and intelligently, if cynically, governed."[36] Another analyst similarly noted Iran's economic malaise, but went even further in concluding that

> Iran has managed to ensure adequate resources for vital war needs. . . . The present standard of living, which is much depressed from the pre-revolutionary peak, . . . can probably be sustained or improved, which reduces the risk of unrest for economic reasons. . . . It [is] unlikely that the Islamic Republic would alter its war policies, or its foreign policies in general, for economic reasons.[37]

A few months later, Iran dropped its long-standing demands for Iraqi reparations from and the removal of Saddam Hussein and accepted an unconditional ceasefire (a decision Khomeini characterized as "more

---

[32] See Tables 3, 8, and 9.

[33] EIU, *Country Profile–Iran* (1988-89), p. 22. Unofficial estimates (including disguised unemployment) were as high as 40 percent; see *NYT*, May 5, 1988, p. 7.

[34] *Economist,* June 25,1988, p. 49.

[35] *NYT,* June 6, 1988, pp. A1, A10.

[36] John Simpson, "Along the Streets of Tehran: Life under Khomeini," *Harper's Magazine* (January 1988), pp. 42-45.

[37] Patrick Clawson, "Islamic Iran's Economic Politics and Prospects," *Middle East Journal* (summer 1988), pp. 386-87.

deadly than taking poison"[38]), underscoring the severity of Iran's economic problems and rising popular discontent. According to official statistics, living standards had fallen 39 percent between 1977 and 1988. Unofficial estimates (corroborated by some official statements) indicate that the drop in living standards was even more severe: a member of parliament was quoted as saying that the real rate of inflation in 1986-87 was 47 percent, double the figure given by the Central Bank.[39]

Khomeini died in June 1989. Two months later, Majlis Speaker Rafsanjani was elected president. He faced an unenviable task. A decade of revolution and war had taken a heavy toll on Iran. According to official estimates, some 160,000 Iranians had been killed during the war.[40] Roughly 1.6 million were homeless, mostly as a result of the 1980-81 Iraqi occupation of parts of western Iran. In addition, Iran had absorbed some 350,000 dissident Iraqis and 2.3 million refugees from the war in Afghanistan.

Aside from the human tragedy, the economic toll included destruction of or serious damage to factories, homes, hospitals, schools, bridges, dams, electric power stations, irrigation networks, oil installations, refineries, ports, and railroads. Official estimates of property damage (not including indirect losses) were $450 billion, although foreign observers believe this figure is highly inflated and put the actual figure at under $200 billion.[41] Unofficial estimates of the cost of repairing only damaged oil installations and refineries were about $15 billion.[42] Reports by foreign observers noted the dismal economic picture:

> Instead of the long promised victory and massive indemnities for war losses [that Khomeini had sought], the regime faces the daunting task of rebuilding a strained economy that has become seriously distorted by war. . . . Economic hardship . . . affect[s] the Iranian public where it really hurts, in recurrent shortages and long queues for poor-quality subsidized food. . . . With Iran spending some two-fifths of its budget on the war, many of the country's most modern, best-equipped plants were turned over to munitions [production] . . . [while others] are operating at 30 percent of capacity [due to] shortages of raw materials, electric power, spare parts, and trained managers and skilled personnel. There is a high rate of absenteeism in factories. Many of the larger factories taken over by the state after the 1979 revolution are heavily overmanned. The key problem is unemployment.[43]

---

[38] *Economist,* July 23, 1988, p. 33-40.

[39] EIU, *Country Report–Iran,* no. 3 (1988), p. 113; Clawson, p. 376.

[40] Unofficial estimates were much higher—about 300,000 killed and 400,000-700,000 wounded, about half of whom were permanently disabled; see EIU, *Country Profile–Iran* (1989-90), p. 90.

[41] Eric Hooglund, "The Islamic Republic at War and Peace," *Middle East Report* (January-February 1989), pp. 4-10. Some suggest that even this figure is inflated; see Clawson, p. 373.

[42] *MEED,* March 3, 1989, pp. 2-4.

[43] *Middle East,* November 1988, pp. 22-24.

The official economic data reflected these problems: compared to 1977, 1988 GDP was down 39 percent (60 percent *per capita*), non-oil GDP was down 26 percent (51 percent *per capita*), living standards were down 39 percent, and investment was down by more than two-thirds.[44]

The clerical regime used the war to explain all or most of the country's economic problems. In reality, many stemmed from the distorting and destructive policies adopted after the revolution.[45] The complex system of multiple exchange rates, price controls and rationing, import licenses, and various direct and indirect subsidies distorted resource allocation and adversely affected production and productivity. The expropriation of various industrial plants and other establishments belonging to the shah, the ruling elite, and others who fled the revolution also had a negative impact. Moreover, these economic policies greatly increased opportunities and inducements for bribery and corruption.[46] Rationed goods sold at controlled prices were often "diverted" by merchants and corrupt officials to the free market, where they were readily available at far higher prices. Similarly, when combined with a foreign exchange allocation at an artificially cheap exchange rate, an import license amounted to "a license to print money."[47] These kinds of activities were far more lucrative than investment in industry or other productive sectors.

One result of these policies was a considerable widening of the already sizable income gap between a small, wealthy elite and the overwhelming majority of poor Iranians who suffered from want and privation. As one Iranian scholar observed, "post-revolutionary Iran has increasingly become polarized into a two-class society of the rich and the poor."[48] The Islamic Republic was supposed to be a state in which improving the welfare of the "deprived" had top priority, but in fact the merchants who control trade and distribution are making fortunes while the deprived suffer badly.[49]

There continue to be deep divisions within the revolutionary regime regarding social and economic policies. Some favor state ownership of industry, strict controls over the private sector, and income redistribution; others are conservatives favoring private enterprise; still others straddle both views. Khomeini often failed to give clear guidance regarding economic policies,[50] and uncertainty about official policies inhibited private (and particularly long-term) investment. Since Khomeini's death

---

[44] See appendices.

[45] *Economist*, April 2, 1988, p. 7.

[46] In 1986, the minister of heavy industry cited an example. The government decreed that domestically produced automobiles would be sold at the artificially low price of 800,000 rials. Those with "connections" pay (i.e., bribe) for the right to purchase a car from the factory, and then make an instant and riskless fortune by immediately reselling it outside the factory gate for the market price, which is three times higher; see Clawson, pp. 384-85.

[47] *Middle East Review*, 1988, p. 69.

[48] Amirahmadi, p. 196.

[49] *MidEast Markets*, May 15, 1989, p. 13.

[50] *Middle East* (January 1989), p. 25; *MEED*, February 10, 1989, pp. 2-3.

in 1989, the disputes within the clerical regime regarding social and economic policies have become even more strident and divisive, often inhibiting the adoption of effective economic policies that would increase national production and productivity.[51]

IRAN'S POST-WAR ECONOMY

The 1988 ceasefire permitted the new regime to focus more intensely on oil production. Foreign exchange earnings from oil exports were crucial to financing imports of machinery, equipment, and raw materials desperately needed to revitalize the economy. According to official Iranian sources, crude oil production rose from 2.6 MBD in 1988 to 3.9 MBD in 1993, the highest level since the 1979 revolution (though far below the peak of 6 MBD in 1976).[52] Other sources indicate that Iranian production was 3.6 MBD in 1993 and remained at that level in 1994.[53] Annual oil export revenues soared from $9.7 billion in 1988 to $12 billion in 1989 and $16-18 billion in 1990-92.

Though partly the result of increased production and exports, the biggest boon to the economy in this period was the 1990-91 Persian Gulf War. Oil prices had been dropping strongly in 1990 until the Iraqi invasion of Kuwait in August of that year—and the subsequent UN embargo on oil exports from Iraq (and Kuwait while under Iraqi occupation)—sharply raised oil prices. For a short while, prices were as high as $35 per barrel. The average price for calendar year 1990 was $22.05 per barrel, 28 percent higher than in 1989. As a result, Iranian oil export revenues rose 49 percent in 1990, before falling somewhat in 1991-92 (but remaining far higher than in 1989).[54]

The oil bonanza was fortuitous for the Rafsanjani regime, which faced the horrendous problems of reconstruction and development. Stimulated by the jump in oil export earnings, GDP increased 34 percent (22 percent *per capita*) between 1989 and 1993.[55] The (relative) windfall of foreign currency earnings allowed Iran to loosen import controls and usher in a comparative flood of consumer goods, machinery, and equipment. Annual commodity imports, which had ranged between $12-13 billion in 1985-89, rocketed to $25 billion in 1991 and only slightly less ($23 billion) the

---

[51] Menashri, pp. 45-57.

[52] See Table 4.

[53] See Table 1. Though this table is based on the Roman calendar (rather than the Muslim calendar used for Iranian figures), this difference hardly explains the wide discrepancies over a number of years. The *Petroleum Economist*'s estimates for Iranian production in recent years are also lower and are close to the estimates of British Petroleum that were the source for Table 1; see *Petroleum Economist* (August 1995), p. 32.

[54] See Tables 5 and 6; International Monetary Fund (IMF), *International Financial Statistics Yearbook*, vol. 47 (Washington, DC: IMF, 1994), p. 169.

[55] See Table 9.

following year. The balance of payments, which had enjoyed a slight surplus of about $300 million in 1990, recorded a massive deficit of $9.4 billion in 1991 and a large (but more modest) deficit of $6.5 billion the year after that.

Oil prices eventually dropped again, however, and by 1993 were lower than in 1989—even when measured in current dollars. When the free market rate of the dollar rose sharply in 1993-94, the government again sharply curtailed imports, which dropped to $12.7 billion, about half their 1991 level.[56] As in the past, this had a negative impact on investment and production, particularly for industry. The widening gaps among the various "official" exchange rates and between these rates and the free market value only exacerbated inefficiencies and provided even more incentives and opportunities for corrupt practices. In 1993, there was a minuscule rise in GDP—when adjusted for population growth, it actually declined—and there are indications that this trend persisted, at least on a *per capita* basis, in 1994 and 1995.

Though imports continued to fall, oil export revenues fell even more rapidly (due mainly to lower oil prices) and the result was persistent current account deficits, rising debt, and in 1992-93 what amounted to national bankruptcy—for the first time, Iran defaulted on its external debts.[57] In early 1995, Central Bank officials stated that Iran's external debt was $27 billion, of which $12.7 billion had been "rescheduled" in 1994.[58] This accumulation of debt was a new phenomenon. Under Khomeini, the Islamic regime had adopted a policy of reduced foreign dependence that compelled it to drastically reduce the $15 billion foreign debt inherited from the shah to $1 billion, despite the massive expenditures associated with the war with Iraq.[59] After the war and the death of Khomeini, however, Rafsanjani's willingness to incur foreign debt in order to accelerate post-war reconstruction and development marked a distinct departure for the Islamic regime.[60]

The Rafsanjani government also appeared to favor a much greater role for the private sector, including foreign private investment. In mid-1991, he declared that Iran was " 'converting from a centralized [wartime] economy . . . to a [more] balanced [peacetime] economy' " and that the "continuation of a state-dominated and subsidized economy would bring ruin."[61] Accordingly, the government reduced subsidies for fuel, cement, and public transportation and phased others out altogether. Between 1991 and 1992, rents doubled. Rafsanjani's efforts at economic liberalization have been marked by a pattern of hesitancy and vacillation, however, and

[56] *MEED*, September 8, 1995, p. 8.
[57] See Table 5.
[58] EIU, *Country Report–Iran*, no. 1 (1995), p. 23.
[59] *Middle East*, July 1993, pp. 13-15.
[60] *Wall Street Journal (WSJ)*, June 28, 1994, pp. A1, A2.
[61] *MEED*, July 26, 1991, pp. 12-13.

when higher prices provoked violent demonstrations, the president appeared to reverse himself:

> Our constitution [adopted after the Islamic Revolution] has entrusted many of the basic and principal industries to the government. . . . Big industries such as aircraft industries, large-scale machine building, and other big industries are governmentalized . . . . In addition, big foundations [*bonyads*], . . . the National Industries Organization, and certain other [enterprises] are in the hands of the government. We are far from entrusting these big sectors to the private sector.[62]

These statements may have been made to reassure the radicals in parliament and the many militant Islamists scattered throughout the bureaucracy (described as "one of the most cumbersome and infuriatingly difficult in the Middle East"[63]), who strongly opposed economic reforms and were intent on sabotaging any changes.[64] But these contradictory statements also tend to deter both domestic and foreign private investment. Rafsanjani's government subsequently renewed ties with international institutions such as the International Monetary Fund (IMF) and World Bank that favor economic liberalization. In 1993 and 1994, it took some steps in the direction of reforming the system of multiple exchange rates and subsidies for food, energy, and other essentials. Once again, the immediate impact of these measures was increased inflation and violent popular reaction, and in 1995 Rafsanjani abandoned most of the reforms. In essence, the reform program has been "subverted, delayed, or blocked by his political opponents within the Islamic regime."[65]

Despite Iran's severe economic and social problems, U.S. government intelligence analyses have consistently concluded that the Islamic government is stable. As recently as February 1997, the acting director of central intelligence told a Senate committee that, even with "ebbing public support for the revolution" and "growing discontent among many Iranians, opposition to clerical rule lacks a charismatic leader or an institutional power base. Moreover, the clerics are adept at burying their differences in the interests of retaining their control."[66] With conservative Majlis Speaker Ali Akbar Nateq Nuri projected to win the May 1997 elections, however, there is little likelihood that the far-reaching economic reforms needed to spur high-level growth will be implemented. Thus, in the absence of a sustained increase in world oil prices, Iran's oil export revenues will continue their long-term decline (at least when adjusted for inflation), thereby compounding its economic difficulties and further undermining its political and social stability.

---

[62] *Iran Focus,* June 1991.

[63] *NYT,* April 8, 1991, p. 7.

[64] Ibid., April 9, 1991, p. A10.

[65] DRI/McGraw-Hill, *World Markets Report–Iran* (May 1995).

[66] Statement by Acting Director of Central Intelligence George J. Tenet to Senate Select Committee on Intelligence, February 5, 1997; see also *NYT,* May 20, 1995, pp. A1, A10.

III

The Oil and Gas Sectors

The discovery of oil in Iran in 1908—and the advent of commercial production by the British-owned Anglo-Persian Oil Company shortly thereafter—preceded oil extraction in Saudi Arabia and other Persian Gulf countries by almost three decades. Negotiations after World War II for a revision of the concession agreement abruptly ended (and Iranian oil production nearly ceased) when Tehran nationalized the Anglo-Persian Oil Company in 1951. Three years later, it awarded a new concession to a consortium of mainly American and British oil companies in exchange for half of the profits. Production rose rapidly from 500,000 barrels per day in 1956 to 3.8 MBD in 1970 and peaked at 6 MBD in 1976.[1]

But Tehran grew increasingly dissatisfied with the 1954 concession agreement and in March 1973 (about six months before the 1973-74 oil crisis) it concluded a new agreement in which the National Iranian Oil Company took over all operations (including refining) and the role of the Anglo-American consortium was reduced to technical adviser and oil export contractor. Between 1974 and 1977, Iran's oil output dropped moderately from 6 to 5.7 MBD.[2] In 1977, Iran accounted for 9 percent of world oil production and an even higher proportion of international trade in oil.

REVOLUTION, WAR, AND THE OIL SECTOR

When the Islamic regime assumed power in February 1979, the limited role of the Anglo-American consortium was terminated altogether.[3] Pre-revolution strikes and violence had reduced oil production and by the end of 1978 oil exports had nearly stopped, creating worldwide panic in the oil markets. Prices rose astronomically in response to the Islamic revolution, in part because buyers feared that it would spread to neighboring Arab countries and reduce their oil production as well.

---

[1] In 1977, Iran produced 5.7 MBD and exported 5 MBD, making it the world's second largest oil exporter behind Saudi Arabia, which exported about 8.5 MBD that year; see Economist Intelligence Unit (EIU), *Quarterly Economic Review/Annual Supplement–Iran* (October 1965), pp. 15-16; British Petroleum, *Statistical Review of World Energy,* June 1995.

[2] See Table 1. Considering that Saudi Arabia and other Middle East producers were successfully raising their output during this period, the reasons for Iran's decline are unclear.

[3] EIU, *Country Profile–Iran* (1991-92), pp. 27-28.

17

The clerical regime resumed oil exports in the spring of 1979, but at a much lower level than had prevailed during the 1973-77 period. This was followed by a steady decline in production from 3.9 MBD in April-June 1979 to a paltry 1.4 MBD in June-August 1980 that made the international oil markets even more nervous. Although the leaders of the revolution had criticized the shah for increasing Iran's dependence on oil, the decline appears to have resulted from technical problems rather than a deliberate policy of reducing oil dependence. The abrupt termination of the concession agreement with the Western consortium—and the general turmoil associated with the revolution—led to a large-scale exodus of Iranian and foreign technical and managerial personnel that adversely affected oil operations and thus the economy as a whole. Despite the 39 percent decline in oil production and consequent drop in exports, however, 1979 oil revenues ($23.4 billion) were about the same as in 1977, due to a precipitous rise in oil prices—also caused by the revolution. By 1980, however, output had declined to 1.5 MBD, reducing export revenues to $11.7 billion and converting a $12 billion balance of payments surplus into a $2.4 billion deficit.[4]

The war with Iraq increased Iran's need for hard currency to finance imports of arms and civilian goods, and thus ideological constraints on excessive oil dependence were quickly discarded. During the first few years of the war, the authorities were quite successful in raising oil production and exports. Despite Iraqi attacks on oil installations, output averaged 2.7 MBD in 1982-83—significantly higher than the abysmally low level of less than 1.5 MBD in 1980-81. The volume of oil exports rose rapidly enough to offset increased domestic consumption caused by the revival of the wartime economy. As world oil prices eroded rapidly during 1982-85 (and then plummeted in 1986), however, export revenues fell drastically from $21.2 billion in 1983 to a dismal $6.3 billion in 1986.[5]

Though prices (and revenues) revived somewhat in 1987-88, they attained only half of the peak levels of 1982-83.[6] Moreover, export revenue figures during this period overstated Iran's foreign currency earnings, because Iraqi attacks on Kharg Island (Iran's main export terminal) and tankers carrying Iranian oil forced Tehran to absorb higher insurance costs to maintain sales. In fact, Iraqi attacks on oil refineries (particularly at Abadan, at the time one of the world's largest refineries) actually forced Iran to *import* refined oil products.[7] In addition to damage inflicted by Iraqi

---

[4] This was also due partly to the war with Iraq, which began in September 1980. See Tables 1, 4, and 5. Non-oil exports during this period were insignificant.

[5] Average oil prices reached a peak worldwide of $36.48 per barrel in 1980, dropped steadily to $26.98 in 1985, and then fell drastically to $13.82 in 1986.

[6] See Tables 4 and 5; see also International Monetary Fund (IMF), *International Financial Statistics Yearbook*, vol. 47 (Washington, DC: IMF, 1994), p. 169. The IMF figures are annual averages for crude oil. The movement of Iranian crude prices is quite similar to that of average world crude oil prices.

[7] Shortly "after the [1988] ceasefire, a British institute estimated war damages to the oil

attacks, the oil fields reportedly also suffered permanent damage from lack of maintenance during the revolution and war.[8]

THE OIL SECTOR SINCE THE WAR

Immediately after the 1988 ceasefire, the Iranian authorities put the highest priority on restoring and expanding oil production capacity, and repairing badly-damaged export terminals and oil refineries. Oil Minister Gholamreza Aqazedeh asserted soon thereafter that productive capacity would be expanded to 4 MBD by the spring of 1989. The ideological call for reducing Iran's dependence on oil—suspended shortly after the revolution due to wartime necessity—was now quietly abandoned. In the fall of 1991, Aqazedeh extended the deadline for reaching this goal by three years (to 1992) and set a new target of 4.5 MBD by 1993.[9] Iran succeeded in raising its oil output from 2.6 MBD in 1988 to about 3.6 MBD by 1992.[10] In 1995, he declared that Iran's capacity had reached 4.1 MBD[11] and would rise to 5.5 MBD (about 85 percent of the pre-revolution level)[12] by the year 2000.[13]

The reasons for these delays were made clear in 1991, when an unnamed French oil executive, commenting on the prospects for an agreement with Iran, stated that the National Iranian Oil Company "has nothing: no personnel, no training, no back-up."[14] Although this was an exaggeration (Iran repaired oil installations damaged during the war with limited foreign assistance),[15] the shortage of skilled labor and capital seriously impeded Iran's efforts to develop its oil potential. The obvious solution—negotiating agreements with foreign oil companies that could provide investment capital, advanced technology, and skilled personnel—runs counter to nationalist sentiments (codified into legal mechanisms) against "foreign exploitation" of Iran's patrimony.

---

facilities at $25 billion"; see *Gulf States Newsletter*, August 22, 1988, p. 13. To put this figure into perspective, annual oil export earnings in 1987-88 averaged about $10 billion; see Table 5.

[8] *MidEast Markets*, March 6, 1989, p. 8.

[9] Ibid., (November 1991), p. 33.

[10] *Petroleum Economist* (November 1995), p. 36.

[11] Industry estimates of Iran's 1995 production were no more than 3.8 MBD; see *Petroleum Intelligence Weekly*, May 29, 1995, p. 6.

[12] *Middle East Economic Digest (MEED)*, June 9, 1995, p. 7.

[13] Others have spoken of returning to the pre-revolution level of 6 or 6.5 MBD by the end of the century; see *Petroleum Economist* (November 1991), p. 33.

[14] *Business Week*, June 10, 1991, p. 52.

[15] Iran has significantly reduced imports of oil products, but was still importing an average of 100,000 barrels per day in recent years; see *MEED*, July 21, 1995, p. 34.

These restrictions apparently do not apply to offshore exploration,[16] which accounted for 11 percent of total production capacity in 1995.[17] Iran spent several years negotiating with the U.S. oil company Conoco to develop two offshore fields until the Clinton administration effectively vetoed the agreement in May 1995 by tightening the U.S. trade embargo on Iran to ban all oil purchases. Some argue that the U.S. embargo will have little effect on Iran because other countries will readily buy its oil and take advantage of profitable investments. Indeed, two months after the Conoco deal fell through, Iran signed a similar deal with the French company Total which is expected to raise production by 120,000 barrels per day by the year 2000,[18] and other companies are also pursuing deals to develop Iran's energy resources, particularly eleven international tenders offered in August 1995.[19] Companies from some forty countries including France, Britain, Italy, Spain, Finland, Canada, and Australia attended a November 1995 conference in Tehran to discuss the Iranian offers.[20] The Islamic regime has held similar meetings to discuss exploration, extraction, and transportation of oil and gas around the Caspian Sea.[21]

Recent reports, however, indicate that many of these projects have been delayed or stalled altogether due to U.S. political and financial pressure.[22] According to the *Washington Post*, none of the eleven tenders has received any bids, and at least two major energy projects with private Australian and Japanese firms have been cancelled (and funding for others delayed).[23] Similarly, Azerbaijan reportedly excluded Iran from an energy consortium at American insistence.[24] In late January 1997, a senior Iranian oil official conceded that investment in Iran's oil and gas sectors was lagging and that U.S. sanctions were partly to blame.[25]

---

[16] *Financial Times (FT)*, May 19, 1995, p. 5.

[17] *MEED*, July 21, 1995, p. 29. This is expected to increase to about 21 percent by 2000, if the oil ministry's projections—which have frequently been overly optomistic—are realized.

[18] Ibid., July 28, 1995, p. 7. Total reportedly contracted with the Irish firm Momentum in April 1996 for a rig to begin drilling; see EIU, *Country Report–Iran*, no. 1 (1996), p. 20.

[19] EIU, *Country Report–Iran*, no. 1 (1996), p. 21; see also U.S. Department of Agriculture (Foreign Agricultural Services), *Report of U.S. Embassy–Abu Dhabi* (April 1995).

[20] EIU, *Country Report–Iran*, no. 1 (1996), p. 22.

[21] Ibid., p. 23. Several of these deals have involved "swaps" of Iranian crude exported from the Gulf in exchange for an equal amount transferred from Caspian littoral states to refineries in northern Iran. Tehran has also agreed in principle to joint ventures with Russia and Azerbaijan.

[22] "U.S. Economic Offensive against Iran's Energy Industry is Bearing Fruit," *Washington Post* (*WP*), March 3, 1997; *FT*, May 16, 1995, p. 8.

[23] "U.S. Economic Offensive," *WP*, March 3, 1997.

[24] EIU, *Country Report–Iran*, no. 1 (1996), p. 23.

[25] "U.S. Economic Offensive," *WP*, March 3, 1997. The article also cites the obstacles created by the Iranian bureaucracy and the fact that the Islamic regime's terms are not as attractive as those offered elsewhere. The initial buy-back terms, for example, would have resulted in returns as low as 5 percent, though these were later revised upward to 20-30 percent; see EIU, *Country Report–Iran*, no. 1 (1996), p. 22.

At the same time, domestic oil consumption has risen very rapidly, due primarily to implicit subsidies that keep the local price of gasoline and other refined oil products extremely low. According to one estimate, domestic fuel prices were held to 10 to 20 percent of international prices in the early 1990s. Even after raising the price of gasoline in 1991, it was still only twenty cents per gallon at the free market exchange rate.[26] The rapid devaluation of the Iranian rial in 1994 effectively lowered the price even further to eight or nine cents per gallon. According to Oil Minister Aqazedeh, fuel subsidies cost the government $6.3 billion in fiscal 1993-94. In view of the financial and technical impediments to significantly expanding oil production, he warned in 1994 that unless domestic oil consumption were strongly curbed, within fifteen years Iran would have no surplus oil to export.[27]

Official Iranian estimates of proven oil reserves are 93 billion barrels, of which 5 billion are offshore. According to Iran's director of exploration, another 1-2 billion barrels will be discovered by the end of the decade, and new technology may eventually permit the recovery of another 20 billion barrels.[28] Other assessments are far less optimistic. According to Amuzegar, proven reserves are actually only 60 billion barrels.[29] Some foreign experts doubt Iran's ability to expand capacity as planned, in part because the lack of proper reservoir maintenance resulted in the permanent loss of some of the original capacity.[30] Another analyst noted that there had been no major discoveries of new oil fields nor sustained application of modern oil recovery techniques such as water and gas injection. "There is therefore no sign of Iran's being able to significantly boost production . . . in coming years," he concluded.[31]

NATURAL GAS

Though Iran's oil reserves are exceeded by those of its Arab neighbors, it is the repository of 14.9 percent of world natural gas reserves—second only to Russia, which has 34.1 percent.[32] The outlook for world gas

---

[26] Jahangir Amuzegar, *Iran's Economy under the Islamic Republic* (London: I.B. Taurus & Co., 1993), p. 254.

[27] *Middle East Economic Survey* (*MEES*), November 14, 1994, p. A13.

[28] *MEED*, July 21, 1995, p. 26.

[29] Amuzegar, p. 229. Even this lower estimate of reserves is substantial, however, approximating those of Venezuela, twice those of the United States, and larger than Mexico's—though far lower than other Gulf states.

[30] *Petroleum Economist*, February 1993, pp. 3-4.

[31] *Gulf States Newsletter*, February 13, 1995, p. 12.

[32] The bulk of Iranian natural gas is what is known as "associated gas"—that is, emitted as a by-product of oil extraction. Thus, high levels of oil output result in high levels of natural gas output. Iran also possesses fields of non-associated (i.e., independent of oil production) gas.

demand is promising. It is preferred over coal and oil due to its lesser environmental impact, and because (unlike oil) gas reserves are widely dispersed geographically and mostly outside the volatile Middle East. Despite this, Iran accounted for only 1.7 percent of world gas production in 1995. The problem is mostly logistical—about 75 percent of the international trade in natural gas is transported via pipelines.[33] In 1994, Russia produced 27.2 percent of total world natural gas, much of it transported to Europe through huge pipelines. Algeria, which has only 2.6 percent of world gas reserves, accounts for 2.4 percent of world production because it uses similar pipelines running under the Mediterranean to deliver gas to the huge European market. Canada, with only 1.6 percent of world gas reserves, accounted for fully 6.5 percent of world gas production because (in addition to the demand generated by its own large economy) it has the advantage of exporting large quantities of gas to the world's largest economy next door.[34]

In 1970 a newly completed pipeline allowed Iran to begin exporting gas to the southern republics of the Soviet Union. In exchange, the Soviets built a large steel mill and other industrial plants in Iran. By 1977, Iranian natural gas production had reached an annual peak of 59.5 billion cubic meters (BCM), of which 24 BCM were consumed domestically, over 9 BCM were exported, and the rest were mostly flared (i.e., burned off) and thus wasted. Shortly after the revolution, however, the Islamic government canceled the pipeline agreement with the Soviet Union in a dispute over price, and gas exports ceased.[35] Local consumption also fell and surplus production was flared.

The clerical regime concluded a new agreement with the Soviets in 1989 and exports resumed in 1990—but at a far lower level than in the 1970s—in exchange for Russian construction of new industrial projects.[36] In view of the meager earnings from gas exports,[37] Iran adopted a policy of maximizing domestic gas consumption in order to free up more oil for export. Its stated goals in 1990-91 were to extend the gas grid throughout the country and double domestic consumption (20-21 BCM in 1989-90) in the first half of the 1990s,[38] which was achieved in 1994.[39]

Iranian officials signed a deal in 1996 to build a gas pipeline to Turkey and thence to Europe, hosted an international gas conference in February

---

[33] Exporting liquefied natural gas (LNG) requires expensive facilities in both the producing and consuming countries.

[34] British Petroleum, *Statistical Review of World Energy* (June 1995), pp. 18-25.

[35] See Table 4.

[36] EIU, *Country Profile–Iran* (1991-92), p. 31.

[37] In 1990, total gas exports were about $200 million, compared to oil export revenues of $17.7 billion; see Table 5.

[38] *Petroleum Intelligence Weekly,* July 1, 1991, p. 9.

[39] The new goal is to reach domestic consumption of 50 BCM by the end of the decade; see EIU, *Country Report–Iran,* no. 2 (1995), p. 18.

1997,[40] and have for many years discussed another line to Pakistan and thence to India. Ultimately, however, logistical difficulties involved in such large-scale projects cast doubt on the economic feasibility of these proposals,[41] and political problems such as Washington's influence on potential partners and Iran's struggle for influence in the newly independent former Soviet republics (not to mention the state of relations between Pakistan and India) only add to the economic obstacles that prevent Tehran from exploiting its very large natural gas reserves. Thus, oil will continue to provide Iran with the bulk of its export earnings in the foreseeable future.

---

[40] Firms from Britain, Italy, Australia, Malaysia, Holland, and France participated, and other conferences are scheduled for April and May; see *MEED,* February 28, 1997, p. 25. Iran has concluded some agreements for gas pipelines to Armenia and the Ukraine, but these are small markets; see EIU, *Country Profile–Iran* (1994-95), p. 29.

[41] *MEED,* October 18, 1991, p. 7; "Natural Gas Markets," *Energy Economist,* no. 104 (June 1990), p. 24; *Middle East Review* (1991-92), p. 60.

IV

Iranian Agriculture: Potential and Reality

During the 1960s, the shah implemented a wide-ranging land reform program that expropriated much of the acreage held by a small number of landowners and redistributed it to the renters and sharecroppers who had been cultivating it. Some 1.8 million tenant farmers became landowners and another 800,000 with disputed titles to the land had their ownership confirmed. Aside from income redistribution, the goal was to give the cultivators the motivation that comes with ownership, particularly with regard to long-term farm investment. The government also improved extension services, expanded agricultural credits, and initiated large dam and irrigation projects. Mechanization was encouraged, and industries related to agriculture—including flour milling, canning, cold storage, and the production of agricultural machinery—were developed.

During 1963-77, the average annual growth rate of agricultural production was a creditable 4.6 percent (1.9 percent *per capita*).[1] Annual production per agricultural worker rose by 3.8 percent during the same period due to mechanization, increased use of fertilizers, improvements in agricultural techniques, higher crop yields, and an increase in the area being irrigated. Though farm production grew more rapidly than population, rapid growth in incomes raised demand for agricultural products, particularly meat, fish, and dairy products. During the 1960s, the agricultural trade balance (exports minus imports) ranged from a small surplus to a small deficit. During the oil boom of 1974-77, however, agriculture's share of non-oil GDP fell from 31 percent to 23 percent.[2] Incomes and demand soared, imports exceeded exports by an annual average of $1.4 billion, and huge agricultural trade deficits emerged.[3]

The leaders of the revolution were highly critical of the shah's agricultural policies, claiming among other things that the plots given to the farmers under the land reform program were less than the minimum necessary for subsistence and that previous technical and financial help to farmers was inadequate. They blamed these policies for an increase in

---

[1] U.S. Department of Commerce, *Foreign Economic Trends–Iran* (December 1982), p. 11; M.G. Majd, "The Oil Boom and Agricultural Development: A Reconsideration of Agricultural Policy in Iran," *Journal of Energy and Development* (autumn 1989), p. 125.

[2] Agriculture is measured here in terms of non-oil GDP because the gap between the highly overvalued official exchange rate and other rates widened in the 1980s, and thus official records of oil revenues in the national accounts effectively reduced oil's contribution to GDP and raised the apparent contribution of other sectors.

[3] See Table 11.

rural poverty that in turn spurred mass migration to the cities and greater dependence on imported food.[4]

POST-REVOLUTION AGRICULTURAL DEVELOPMENT

Once in power, the clerical regime declared that priority would be given to the agriculture sector in order to raise rural living standards, reduce rural-urban migration, and achieve food self-sufficiency. Many landlords joined the exodus of professionals and other skilled workers in the early years of the revolution, and their replacements often lacked the expertise to manage the farms. Others tried to reclaim land expropriated under the shah, leading to violent clashes with the peasants to whom it had been given.[5] By the end of 1981, the authorities succeeded in ending these clashes,[6] and in 1982 the Majlis passed the Land Reform Act, which resulted in limited land redistribution but led to uncertainty regarding land tenure. Though only 3 percent of the cultivated land was redistributed to poor farmers during the 1980s, as much as one-third of total farm land came under dispute, adversely affecting production in some areas. [7] Uncertainty discouraged investment in irrigation and other such improvements.[8] According to one economic journal, "[a]griculture has yet to recover from the damage done during the 1970s, the flight of the landlords in 1979-80, and the uncertainties surrounding government policies after the 1980 land reform."[9]

Official policy during the 1980s was to offer farmers a wide range of incentives—such as subsidies for farm inputs and high procurement prices for many farm products—in order to increase agricultural production, reduce food imports, and conserve scarce foreign exchange. This was made easier by the fact that agriculture was less dependent on imported inputs than other sectors of the economy such as industry, which often operated far below capacity because of the shortages of imported raw materials, spare parts, and other inputs during the 1980s. The U.S. Department of Agriculture estimated that Iran's agricultural production rose by an average annual rate of 3.9 percent between 1977 and 1989, roughly approximating the rate of population growth. Iranian estimates of the average annual growth rate of value-added in agriculture during the

---

[4] Jahangir Amuzegar, *Iran's Economy under the Islamic Republic* (London: I.B. Taurus & Co., 1993), p. 180.

[5] Though many clerics had opposed the shah's land redistribution as "un-Islamic" because it undermined the right to private property, some landless peasants cited Islam's notions of equity and social justice as a justification for seizing large land holdings.

[6] Hooshang Amirahmadi, *Revolution and Economic Transition: The Iranian Experience* (Albany, NY: State University of New York Press, 1990), pp. 27-28.

[7] U.S. Department of Commerce, *Foreign Economic Trends–Iran* (December 1982), p. 11.

[8] *Economist*, February 11, 1989, p. 56.

[9] Economist Intelligence Unit (EIU), *Country Profile–Iran* (1994-95), p. 16.

same period were 4.3 percent.[10] In addition to the war with Iraq and the uncertainties surrounding land tenure, the often haphazard distribution of seed, fertilizer, and other farm inputs during the 1980s contributed to the lower rate of agricultural production growth in 1977-89 as compared to 1963-77.[11] According to official statistics, there was a significant improvement (due in part to more favorable weather conditions) in the agricultural sector in 1989-93, with production rising by an average annual rate of 7.9 percent and annual value-added rising by 6.5 percent.

In the 1980s, the growth rate in agricultural production was far lower than in the pre-revolution decade, but other sectors suffered greater damage from revolutionary turmoil and the war with Iraq. Though agriculture in the areas adjacent to Iraq suffered serious damage, agriculture's share of non-oil GDP rose from 23 percent in 1977 to 31 percent in 1989 and 34 percent in 1993.[12] The growth stems not from agriculture's strong performance in 1977-89, but rather the relatively weak performance of other sectors, in which production actually declined.

Estimates of the agricultural labor force are notoriously inaccurate (particularly in less developed countries) due to wide seasonal swings and the fact that unpaid family labor is often underreported. Official Iranian census figures show that the agricultural segment of the labor force dropped from 48 percent in 1970 to 37 percent in 1977, to 27 percent in 1982, and remained at about the same level in 1986.[13] A 1994 World Bank study reported higher estimates, stating that agriculture accounts for one-third of total employment.[14] Iran's Ministry of Agriculture claims that the relatively high growth rate of agriculture in recent years has raised rural incomes to 70 percent of urban incomes, reducing the wide gap between the two. While conceding that this was due to lower urban incomes, the ministry argues that real rural incomes have increased in absolute as well as relative terms.[15] The average annual agricultural trade deficit appears to have increased, however, from $1.7 billion in 1987-89 to $2 billion in 1990-92.[16]

---

[10] See Tables 9 and 11. The latter estimate appears to be somewhat high, given the substantial growth in the use of fertilizers and other subsidized inputs during this period. One would therefore expect a slower rate of growth in value-added than gross production.

[11] EIU, *Country Profile–Iran* (1994-95), p. 22.

[12] See Table 9.

[13] EIU, *Country Profile–Iran* (1991-92), p. 10; Majd, p. 128. U.S. Department of Agriculture estimates of agriculture's share of the labor force in the 1980s are significantly higher—34.5 percent in 1982 and 30.6 percent in 1986, dropping to 27.7 percent in 1992; see Table 11.

[14] World Bank, *Services for Agriculture and Rural Development–Islamic Republic of Iran*, vol. 1 (1994).

[15] EIU, *Country Report–Iran*, no. 1 (1995), p. 21.

[16] See Table 11. The figures are in current U.S. dollars. Overall, the International Monetary Fund (IMF) Food Price Index for each period is almost unchanged—and the price index of Iran's international trade in agricultural products is assumed to approximate that of the IMF Food Price Index; see IMF, *International Financial Statistics Yearbook*, vol. 47 (Washington, DC: IMF, 1994), p. 171.

In a 1991 interview, President Rafsanjani was quite candid in his evaluation of the problems facing Iranian agriculture:

> Our agriculture has not been efficient. Our dry [unirrigated] farming has low yields, ploughing is not done in the manner it should be. . . . [Fertilizers] are not offered [by the state] to the farmers at the right time. . . . Our water [resources] are untapped . . . . Even after crops are picked, much of it is lost because of the distance between the fields and the barns and depots.[17]

Iran's agricultural productivity is about "one-third of the level of developed countries" and annual farm output is "considerably below the country's potential."[18] The state has been deficient in instructing farmers in the latest techniques, as well as investing in dams, irrigation, storage facilities, roads, and other infrastructure essential to the agricultural sector. The inefficiency of state enterprises in providing adequate and timely deliveries of fertilizers and pesticides adversely affects productivity. According to one estimate, as much as one-third of Iran's crops are lost because of the lack of adequate storage and transportation facilities.[19]

Under Rafsanjani, however, there have been some important agricultural policy reforms. Farmers are no longer obliged to sell their produce to the state, and some price controls and subsidies for inputs and consumer goods were reduced or phased out altogether.[20] The 1995-99 Five-Year Economic Development Plan has even more ambitious goals for agriculture, including a net food surplus by the final year of the plan and greater emphasis on mechanization and food processing. The minister of agriculture boasted that Iran "now produce[s] 84 percent of our food requirements as compared with 75 percent five years ago."[21] Foreign observers are more skeptical. A U.S. Department of Agriculture assessment stated that about 20 percent of Iran's food requirements are supplied via the United Arab Emirates and that, despite efforts to increase domestic agricultural production, "Iran is likely to remain dependent for the foreseeable future on imports for a significant part of its basic food needs."[22]

The 1995-99 plan sets forth ambitious goals for agriculture with the emphasis on improved efficiency and the development of agro-industries.

---

[17] *Iran Focus* (June 1991).

[18] Amuzegar, p. 178.

[19] U.S. Department of Agriculture (Foreign Agricultural Services), *Report of U.S. Embassy–Abu Dhabi* (April 1995).

[20] World Bank, *Services for Agriculture and Rural Development–Islamic Republic of Iran*, vol. 1 (1994).

[21] *Middle East Economic Digest* (*MEED*), February 10, 1995, pp. 8-15.

[22] *Report of U.S. Embassy–Abu Dhabi* (April 1995). The *Financial Times* reports that Iran imports 30-50 percent of its food requirements; see *Financial Times/ Survey–Iran*, February 8, 1993, p. vi. The assessment of the U.S. Department of Agriculture refers only to Iranian food imports via the United Arab Emirates; the *Financial Times* refers to total Iranian food imports.

The potential, in terms of land and water, exists. About 40 percent of the country's water capacity remains unutilized or underutilized. As of 1995, some thirty large dams (and numerous smaller ones) were under construction. Two particularly large dams require considerable technical help from foreign companies. These larger projects are being partly financed by concessionary loans from Japan. The goal is to expand the area under irrigation and increase water supplies for the rapidly growing urban sector.[23] If the authorities pursue policies favorable to agricultural production, allocate the resources necessary to significantly improve infrastructure, and instruct farmers in modern agricultural techniques, the goals of the new plan can—for the most part—be realized.

---

[23] *MEED,* July 28, 1995, p. 26; *Middle East* (July-August 1995), p. 20.

V

Iranian Industry

Iran has long been known for its handicrafts—particularly hand-woven carpets, rugs, metalware, ceramics, and jewelry. Beginning in the 1920s, the government promoted modern manufacturing by offering cheap loans, tax concessions, tariff protection, and other inducements. Industries were established in food processing, textiles, and building materials such as cement. During the 1960s and 1970s there was a major drive to develop "heavy industry." In addition to exporting natural gas to the Soviet Union in exchange for the construction of a steel mill, Iran made agreements with Romania and Czechoslovakia involving the establishment of machine tool and other industries. American, British, French, Italian, and other Western firms were actively involved in building Iran's industrial sector, setting up joint ventures with Iranian public and private enterprises including petrochemical facilities, an aluminum smelter, and plants for assembling vehicles, radios, televisions, and various other electrical appliances. Perhaps the most ambitious project was the construction of a massive petrochemical complex by a Japanese firm at Bandar Shahpur (later renamed Bandar Khomeini) to produce fertilizers, sulfur, and other products. The project was nearly finished when the Islamic revolution (and associated turmoil) hampered its completion. Ultimately, Iraqi bombings inflicted heavy damage on the complex.[1]

Between 1970 and 1977, annual output in what the Iranian statistics bureau calls "large manufacturing establishments" (those employing ten or more workers) advanced by a rapid 15.8 percent and annual employment in this sector increased 6.7 percent, indicating a sizable growth in labor productivity (i.e., output per worker). During this period, the annual rate of growth for industry as a whole (including handicrafts, small workshops, and mining) averaged 11.3 percent.[2] According to one study, Iran

> has a quite exceptional supply of appropriate labor for the development of industry. . . . Few industrializing countries have Iran's advantage . . . [of having] large numbers [of workers who] have for a long time worked in handicraft industries . . . . [and] a steady growth of workshops making articles of more common consumption—cooking utensils, clothes, shoes, [and] furniture . . . . Iran is already highly urbanized, yet without much urban unemployment. It is developing rapidly, yet without shortages of skilled and educated personnel so serious as to retard development.[3]

---

[1] Economist Intelligence Unit (EIU), *Country Profile–Iran* (1991-92), pp. 33-34.

[2] Central Bank of Iran, *Annual Report,* various issues.

[3] Walter Elkan, "Employment, Education, Training, and Skilled Labor in Iran," *Middle East*

There were, however, increasing problems impeding further progress in promoting industrialization. Though Iran may have had a larger pool of skilled labor than most developing countries, the establishment of larger, more sophisticated and capital-intensive industries in the 1970s required a cadre of highly trained technical and especially managerial personnel that (compared to the advanced industrialized countries) were in relatively short supply in both the public and private sectors in Iran.[4] Furthermore, the pace of industrialization was far more rapid than in most developing countries simply because Iran had the advantage of massive oil revenues.

Developing countries usually initiate their industrialization by means of import substitution, but must eventually adopt and promote strong export promotion policies to develop mature and dynamic industries. The discipline imposed by international competition encourages efficiency. Under the shah, Iran achieved high rates of growth in industrial production by erecting unusually strong protection from foreign competition through either prohibitive tariffs, quantitative restrictions, or both. This highly protectionist policy of import substitution rather than export promotion—effectively subsidized by oil revenues—guaranteed industry a captive domestic market but tended to discourage improvements in efficiency and quality, and thereby impaired the ability of Iranian industry to compete in the international export market.[5] Iran barely passed beyond the first stage of industrialization.

REVOLUTION, WAR, AND THE INDUSTRIAL SECTOR

By 1977, rising inflation and the shortage of skilled labor began to affect all sectors of the economy. These problems were exacerbated by the widespread industrial unrest that marked the final two years of the shah's reign. As a result, industrial output declined by one-third between 1976 and 1979. The deterioration of the political situation gave rise to a cycle of disinvestment, even before the revolutionary government took power in February 1979 and "[w]holesale nationalization of industry after the revolution turned disinvestment into the flight of both capital and human resources, leaving Iran's still developing industrial base crippled."[6]

Journal (spring 1977), pp. 186-87.

[4] Andrew G. Carey and Jane Perry Clark Carey, "Industrial Growth and Development Planning in Iran," *Middle East Journal* (winter 1975), p. 14.

[5] In extreme cases, value added (measured in international prices) was negative; see Kamal A. Hammeed and Margaret N. Bennett, "Iran's Future Economy," *Middle East Journal* (autumn 1975), pp. 423-25.

[6] EIU, *Country Profile–Iran* (1994-95), p. 31. Figures for the national accounts indicate that non-oil industry declined by 14 percent in 1977. The index of production by large manufacturing establishments, however, shows an increase of 12 percent in 1977, followed by a sharp decline in 1978. Given that most "non-oil industry" *is* manufacturing, it is difficult to reconcile the two estimates for 1977; see Table 9.

The political climate and excesses during the early years of the revolution

> led to a massive exodus of industrial entrepreneurs, managers, and skilled workers as well as a large-scale flight of capital. The freezing of Iranian assets abroad, Western economic sanctions, and hostile government policies toward multinational corporations resulted in a departure of foreign specialists and the cessation of foreign investment. Inexperienced new managers, labor disputes, and disruptive meddling by members of revolutionary *komitehs* [Islamic cadres] established in each factory further reduced output. The situation was aggravated by the Iran-Iraq War, which damaged and destroyed production facilities.[7]

In mid-1979, parliament passed a law declaring state ownership of all basic and "strategic" industries—oil and gas, railways, electric power, fishing, automobile manufacturing, shipbuilding, and metals industries. These enterprises were either taken over by the state directly or handed over to the newly created *bonyads*, which were to run these enterprises and use the profits to support poor people, widows, orphans, and other worthy causes. As a result, heavy industry and much of light industry now belongs to the public sector (small-scale handicraft industries and workshops remained private), and is overseen by new "ideologically correct" but often incompetent government-appointed managers.[8] Like the shah, the new regime gave domestic industry strong protection against imports.[9]

After many years of rapid growth, output by large manufacturing establishments that became part of the public sector after the revolution declined 8 percent during 1977-80. During the same three-year period, however, employment in manufacturing increased by 13 percent as the managers of these enterprises followed government orders to minimize overt unemployment.[10] This costly policy meant that many of the plants had to be subsidized by the public treasury. In many respects, however, the Islamic Republic's program for rapid industrialization—emphasizing heavy industry—was similar to the last decade of the shah's rule. Oil revenues are crucial to financing the program. When oil revenues rise (as they did in 1982-84 and 1990-92), Iran can afford to import production inputs and the economy—and particularly industry—booms. When oil revenues decline (as in 1993), imports are tightened, industrial production falls sharply,[11] and the economy goes into a recession.

---

[7] Jahangir Amuzegar, "The Iranian Economy Before and After the Revolution," *Middle East Journal* 46, no. 3 (summer 1992), p. 419.

[8] Hooshang Amirahmadi, *Revolution and Economic Transition: The Iranian Experience* (Albany, NY: State University of New York Press, 1990), p. 281.

[9] Sohrab Behdad, "Foreign Exchange Gap, Structural Constraints, and the Political Economy of Exchange Rate Determination," *International Journal of Middle East Studies* (February 1988), p. 12.

[10] See Table 9.

[11] See Tables 5 and 9.

Thus, despite the September 1980 Iraqi invasion and subsequent bombings, industrial output improved slightly in the early 1980s. The war spurred the clerical regime to raise oil output, and higher oil export earnings in 1982-83 allowed the government to loosen import controls. Total merchandise imports—which reached a peak of $16.7 billion in 1977 under the shah and then fell to $10.9 billion in 1980—climbed to $18 billion in 1983.[12] Much of the increase consisted of machinery and equipment, raw materials, and spare parts for industry (which imports some 70 percent of its total inputs). Industrial output (including handicrafts, small workshops, mining, and electricity) rose 93 percent between 1979 and 1985, and manufacturing output (by plants with ten or more workers) rose 76 percent during the same period.[13]

When oil export revenues subsequently declined due to intensive Iraqi attacks on Iranian oil installations and lower world oil prices, manufacturing output declined by one-third between 1984 and 1988[14] (though employment in this sector fell by only 4 percent, as the government instructed plant managers to retain large numbers of redundant workers).[15] In addition, the priority given to military industries reduced resources available to civilian enterprises. Many industrial plants were diverted to the manufacture of machine guns, mortars, ammunition, and other military equipment.[16] The larger munitions plants were state owned, but there was extensive subcontracting to private workshops. These factories were given the highest priority in terms of resource allocation (including scarce foreign exchange), and many worked around the clock in three shifts to meet demand for military equipment.

One report described the whole of Iranian industry in the second half of the 1980s as being "in dire straits; lack of spare parts, power cuts, overmanning, strikes, and poor management have combined to reduce output."[17] Another noted that

> There is a serious conflict between the managers and workers who complain about low wages, which are eaten away by inflation. Absenteeism is common and strikes are not uncommon. According to official estimates, industry was operating at only 50 percent of capacity in 1984, declining to 40 percent in 1988.[18]

Unofficial estimates of industrial output were as low as 20-30 percent of capacity.[19] The head of the state-owned Industrial Development and

---

[12] See Table 5.

[13] See Table 9.

[14] According to independent observers, the decline in output was much larger than official estimates indicated; see EIU, *Country Profile–Iran* (1989-90), p. 34.

[15] See Tables 5 and 9.

[16] *Middle East Economic Digest* (*MEED*), May 2, 1987, p. 11; *Middle East* (April 1988), p. 18.

[17] *Middle East Review* (1987), p. 93.

[18] *MEED*, July 14, 1989, p. 12.

[19] Amirahmadi, p. 281.

Renovation Organization, which controlled some 120 factories accounting for 80 percent of the output of heavy industry, asserted that the economy "was in its worst shape ever."[20] Many if not most public sector industries survived only by virtue of "huge" state subsidies.[21]

INDUSTRY SINCE THE IRAN-IRAQ WAR

Following the 1988 ceasefire, massive funds were needed to make up for the decade of neglected development (1978-88). In addition to capital and labor flight and the physical destruction wrought by the war, other factors inhibited industrial growth. Inefficient public sector enterprises accounted for about 70 percent of total industrial output.[22] Government price controls and exchange rates were often arbitrary (especially for the private sector), providing considerable room for bribery and corruption but little incentive to improve efficiency and reduce costs.[23] As a result, the private sector had invested little in industry since the revolution and focused instead on trade and real estate investment.[24]

Once again, growth was fueled by a surge in oil export revenues, particularly when oil prices rose sharply in response to the 1991 Persian Gulf War. The resultant influx of production inputs allowed Iran to utilize previously idle capacity and led to a major expansion of industrial output. Manufacturing output (measured by value added) increased 50 percent from 1987 to 1991, and industrial production increased 150 percent by 1992.[25] The increase in *value added* to industrial output, however, was a mere 5 percent in 1992—less than 2 percent *per capita*. The 1989-93 Five-Year Plan set a target of 14.3 percent increase in average annual industrial production.[26] Ultimately, it amounted to a considerably lower 9.5 percent.[27] Overall, the plan stressed the development of heavy industry, with the strongest activity in petrochemicals. Development in this sector closely followed the plan, with annual petrochemical production rising from less than 1 million tons in 1987 to 8 million tons in 1994 (and exports as high as $250 million[28]) before falling to 7.5 million tons in fiscal 1995.[29]

---

[20] *MEED*, July 21, 1989, p. 17.

[21] *Middle East* (August 1985), p. 27.

[22] *MidEast Markets*, May 20, 1991, p. 6.

[23] The so-called "cost plus" price is supposed to comprise the cost of manufacturing plus a marginal fee.

[24] *Middle East Review* (1990), p. 71.

[25] See Table 9.

[26] Jahangir Amuzegar, *Iran's Economy under the Islamic Republic* (London: I.B. Taurus & Co., 1993), p. 282.

[27] See Table 9.

[28] EIU, *Country Profile–Iran* (1995-96), p. 36; *MEED*, April 28, 1995, p. 17.

[29] It had been projected to reach 10 million tons by early 1996, and 8.5 million tons the following year; see EIU, *Country Profile–Iran* (1996-97), p. 24.

Rafsanjani's election as president in 1989 led to some important policy changes, including liberalization of price controls for many products, a reduction in the number of official exchange rates (with an ultimate goal of a single realistic exchange rate), and an end to the practice of requiring exporters of non-oil products to surrender foreign currency at an absurdly low official rate. Under a program announced in 1991, some 400 state-owned companies were to be sold to the private sector within two years. Domestic investors were allowed to purchase up to 34 percent equity, with foreign investors limited to 25 percent equity. The companies to be privatized were generally small and medium-sized firms, including some of those that were nationalized after the revolution. The government excluded from the privatization plans what the minister of industry referred to as "strategic heavy industries."[30]

One interesting innovation was a plan to seek foreign investment to develop some Persian Gulf islands as free trade and industrial zones and others as tourist attractions. Kish Island was developed under the shah as a resort for rich Arabs and Europeans and is still equipped with a first-class airport, modern communications facilities, and other vital infrastructure. Qeshm Island has large reserves of natural gas that were offered to foreign investors at about one-third of international prices. The government offered to exempt the island from foreign currency restrictions, as well as business and personal taxes, that apply to mainland Iran. The goal was to develop Qeshm into the "biggest industrial base west of Japan and east of Europe."[31] Initial construction on an international airport there began in January 1996.[32]

In addition to domestic and non-Iranian foreign investment, Rafsanjani called upon merchants, industrialists, and bankers who had fled during and after the revolution to return to Iran and reclaim their nationalized properties, promising to dismiss any legal charges against them and offering low-cost loans for the promotion of non-oil exports. A few returned to Iran, but most remained fearful.[33] Despite Rafsanjani's relatively liberal economic policies, the private sector was hesitant to make long-term investments. Potential investors reacted warily to a 1990 government offer to sell some state-owned mines due to uncertainty about access to adequate electric power and foreign exchange needed to import machinery and spare parts.[34] A 1993 World Bank report described Iran's

---

[30] EIU, *Country Report–Iran*, no. 2 (1991), p. 15; *MEED*, May 1, 1992, p. 5.

[31] *MEED*, March 1, 1991; *Middle East Review* (1991-92), p. 62.

[32] EIU, *Country Report–Iran*, no. 1 (1991), p. 25.

[33] One Iranian living in the United States expressed concerns about getting out of Iran after reclaiming his property. "The Central Bank can issue me a permit to leave the country," he told the *New York Times*, "but it's worthless because I can be prevented from leaving Tehran airport [by] seven different" government agencies that maintain "watch lists" of dissident Iranians; see *New York Times* (*NYT*), June 2, 1991, p. 8.

[34] *Wall Street Journal* (*WSJ*), April 12, 1990, p. A10. Between 1988 and 1993, electric power increased by an annual average of 9.8 percent, compared to 8.7 percent over the previous

industrial sector as "especially constrained by excessive regulation; foreign exchange controls, market deficiencies, and dominance of the public sector, while the private sector is dormant."[35] Industrialists complained that employment laws favored labor: wages and salaries were not usually tied to efficiency and productivity, and dismissals of redundant workers were hampered by government regulations.[36]

By 1994, the government had effectively abandoned plans for significant additional privatization, due to strong parliamentary resistance to the sale of major state companies, legal complications concerning the ownership of nationalized industries expropriated by the *bonyads*,[37] and fear that privatization would lead to large-scale dismissals of redundant workers. Other economic reforms were actually reversed[38]; in an attempt to combat inflation, the government *expanded* the list of price-controlled goods in 1995 to include cars, electrical appliances, various foods and beverages, and construction materials, and increased the penalties for violating price restrictions. It set up hundreds of mobile courts to try merchants for price gouging.[39]

In September 1995, the governor of the Central Bank announced balance of payments figures for fiscal 1994-95 (ending March 20, 1995), the third consecutive year of "import compression." The data indicated that imports had been drastically reduced from $19.3 billion to $12.7 billion.[40] This implies serious hardships for the economy as a whole and industry in particular, and indeed industrial output—which had climbed from less than 50 percent of capacity in 1993 to 60 percent of capacity in 1994—receded again in 1995.[41]

The 1995-99 Five-Year Plan called for greater emphasis on non-oil industrial exports, especially petrochemicals, mining products, steel production, agro-industries, and textiles in addition to traditional exports such as carpets. A Western press report about new technology developed by a team of Iranian engineers at a steel mill in Isfahan described the scientists as part of "a new generation of engineers and managers who have created pockets of excellence and innovation within Iranian industry

---

decade; see Table 4. Though this was a distinct improvement, chronic shortages of electricity caused by war damage, poor maintenance, and the inability to complete major infrastructure projects sometimes led to blackouts and other severe industrial problems during periods of peak demand; see EIU, *Country Profile–Iran* (1994-95), p. 29.

[35] World Bank, *Industry and Mining Sector Report no. 10867–IRN* (March 1993). Private industries (mostly small-scale workshops) receive no support from the public sector.

[36] EIU, *Country Report–Iran,* no. 1 (1994), p. 19.

[37] *Economist,* September 25, 1993, p. 58.

[38] Ibid., January 21, 1995, p. 42; EIU, *Country Report–Iran,* no. 4 (1994), p. 17.

[39] In a January 1995 sermon, Ayatollah Janati referred to merchants who violate price controls as "blood-sucking capitalists [who] should be whipped. People who are drunk with money only understand the language of the whip"; see *MEED,* February 10, 1995, p. 21.

[40] Ibid., September 8, 1995, p. 8. See Table 5.

[41] Ibid., August 18, 1995, p. 5.

during sixteen years of economic hardship" since the revolution. The report quoted a Western steel executive, however, who cautioned that "if the Iranians wish to compete [in the world market], they would have to team up with a foreign company."[42] Similarly, financial difficulties have impeded swifter progress in expanding production of aluminum.[43]

In 1995, there were reportedly $4.6 billion in applications for foreign investment in the free-trade zones, primarily in petrochemicals, refineries, fertilizers, steel, power stations, hotels, and housing.[44] China alone concluded about $1 billion worth of agreements with Iran in 1995, for projects ranging from power generation, cement, paper, glass, shipbuilding, zinc, copper, and Iran's ambitious dam-building projects. Beijing will be paid in oil as well as non-oil products.[45] Russia was also negotiating in early 1996 to build a 1,000-Mw power plant and factories for assembling motorcycles and Ilyushin aircraft in Iran.[46] And the National Petrochemical Company formed a series of partnerships with foreign firms to begin work on projects worth an estimated $3.3 billion.[47]

But—as with the oil and gas projects—whether these applications and negotiations yield as actual investments still remains to be seen. Chinese news reports in December 1995 claimed that work on the nuclear power plant at Bushehr had been suspended due to lack of funding.[48] Though the completed projects (many of which are being built by foreign contractors) will be managed by Iranian personnel, many are capital-intensive and will do little to reduce current unemployment.[49]

The failure to attract large-scale private investment implies even greater dependence on the public sector and oil revenues, which were lower in the mid-1990s—even when measured in current dollars (i.e., not adjusted for inflation)—than in the mid-1970s and are unlikely to rise significantly in the coming years. In addition to huge oil and gas reserves, Iran is well endowed with a wide range of mineral resources including chromate, lead, kaolin, uranium, cobalt, zinc, ferrous oxide, iron, coal, manganese, tin, tungsten, gold, and copper reserves estimated to be second only to those of Chile.[50] But these resources have hardly been exploited. Barring (unlikely) radical changes in economic policies, Iran's dependence on oil will continue into the indefinite future.

---

[42] Ibid., February 24, 1995, pp. 2-3.

[43] EIU, *Country Report–Iran*, no. 2 (1995), p. 20.

[44] *MEED*, January 20, 1995; February 17, 1995, p. 6; EIU, *Country Report–Iran*, no. 1 (1996), p. 25.

[45] Ibid., June 16, 1995, p. 23.

[46] EIU, *Country Report–Iran*, no. 1 (1991), p. 25.

[47] Ibid.

[48] Ibid.

[49] Ibid., no. 2 (1991), p. 5; and no. 4 (1991), p. 5.

[50] Ibid., *Country Profile–Iran* (1994-95), p. 24.

VI

The Economic Burden of the Military

Under the shah, military expenditures rose very rapidly after the 1973 oil crisis produced windfall oil export revenues. Military spending as a percentage of GNP rose from an annual average of 8-9 percent in 1970-73 to 15 percent in 1974-78. This was reflected in arms imports (largely from the United States and Britain), which rose from $160 million in 1970 to $2.6 billion in 1977, and then fell to $2.1 billion in 1978. The Islamic regime initially cut back sharply on military spending, particularly purchases of sophisticated equipment. Arms imports dropped sharply to $1.5 billion in 1979 and $420 million in 1980.[1]

THE ECONOMIC IMPACT OF THE WAR WITH IRAQ

The September 1980 Iraqi attack reversed the decline in Iran's military spending. During the initial years of the war, the Islamic regime drew on stockpiles of weaponry inherited from the shah, but according to the U.S. Arms Control and Disarmament Agency (ACDA), as the war dragged on annual average arms imports rose from $1.1 billion in 1981-83 to $2.3 billion in 1984-88, an annual average of 1.5 billion.[2] Among the highest estimates of Iran's total defense burden during the war is 20 percent of GDP (including both domestic and military expenditures, arms imports, and allocations for reconstruction).[3] By comparison, the U.S. defense burden during World War II was about 40 percent of GDP.[4] But the United States suffered hardly any direct damage to its civilian economy, whereas the war with Iraq caused severe direct and indirect damage to Iran's economy, due mainly to the former's air superiority. According to another

---

[1] See Table 2. At the same time, however, the Islamic regime established a praetorian volunteer militia known as the Revolutionary Guard that competed with the regular armed forces, which were considered politically suspect because of their association with the shah. The Guard "formed in effect parallel armies, air forces, and even navies, causing intense competition and wastage of resources." See *Middle East Review* (1990), pp. 68-69.

[2] Others estimate Iran's average annual arms imports during the war at $2 billion; see *Middle East Economic Digest* (*MEED*), April 17, 1989, p. 27.

[3] The burden was particularly onerous during the final years of the war (1986-88), when oil revenues plummeted as a consequence of both lower world oil prices and a smaller volume of oil exports due to Iraqi bombings of Iranian oil installations. Arms imports absorbed fully one-quarter of Iran's oil export revenues in this period; see Tables 2 and 5.

[4] Patrick Clawson, "Islamic Iran's Economic Politics and Prospects," *Middle East Journal* (summer 1988), p. 375.

estimate, the war cost Iran about $90 billion in direct damages (i.e., excluding indirect damages such as loss of production in oil and other sectors, neglect of infrastructure, and loss of further development[5]), which is roughly equivalent to Iran's total oil export revenues from 1989 to 1994.

Estimates of these kinds vary because figures regarding Iran's military forces and their economic burden are shrouded in secrecy. Arms imports, for example, are mostly or totally off budget. In addition, government appeals during the war with Iraq reportedly yielded sizable "voluntary" contributions to the war effort that did not appear in published figures. As a result, there is often a wide gap between the figures for national defense stated in the official budgets and those mentioned or alluded to by various ministers in parliamentary debates. In the debate on the 1987 budget, for example, the minister of planning and budget stated that expenditures for the war with Iraq "rose from 18 percent of the general budget in 1980 to 32 percent in 1986"—equivalent to an increase from 6.2 percent of GDP in 1980 to 7.1 percent in 1986. These figures are hardly credible for a country engaged in a bitter war during that period, and indeed the minister later added that the figures for national defense presented in the budget "are only a portion of the actual war expenditures."[6]

Similarly, in presenting the 1987 budget to Iran's parliament, Prime Minister Mir Hossein Mousavi stated that the figures given for defense spending "are only a portion of actual war expenditures, as other resources of executive bodies [were] also deployed. [Some military expenditures are] . . . not stated in any official figures or statistics."[7] According to the 1987 budget, defense spending was equivalent to 2.2 percent of GDP. Mousavi, however, stated that war-related expenditures accounted for 41 percent of the total 1987 budget—an amount equivalent to 7 percent of GDP.[8] But even the higher figure is an understatement; ACDA estimated Iran's military expenditures at 10.3 percent of GNP in 1986 and 8.7 percent in 1987, and also noted that these estimates may only partially (if at all) include arms purchases abroad.[9]

In purely quantitative terms, the mobilization and expansion of the armed forces and military-related industries during the war with Iraq created no significant problems for the civilian economy. According to

---

[5]   Shahram Chubin, "Iran's Strategic Aims and Constraints" in ed. Patrick Clawson, *Iran's Strategic Intentions and Capabilities* (Washington, DC: National Defense University, 1994), p. 87.

[6]   Hooshang Amirahmadi, *Revolution and Economic Transition: The Iranian Experience* (Albany, NY: State University of New York Press, 1990), pp. 165-66. The Ministry of Planning was converted in August 1989 to the Plan and Budget Organization.

[7]   Ibid.

[8]   Ibid., p. 166.

[9]   Military-related imports are recorded in Iranian accounts at the lowest official exchange rate (i.e., the fewest rials per dollar), which have at times in the past decade been 10 or even 5 percent of the free market rate. Thus, even when included in the budget, military-related imports are grossly understated.

ACDA estimates, the armed forces expanded from 247,000 personnel in 1981-83 to 344,000 in 1984-87. In fact, the mobilization was much greater: ACDA estimates apparently exclude the Revolutionary Guards, a separate force that according to one estimate numbered 300,000 by the end of the war.[10] The ratio of Iranians in the armed forces rose slightly during the war from less than six per thousand in 1981-83 to somewhat over seven in 1984-87.[11] Although Iran had more than ample unskilled labor for its civilian economy and the bulk of those in the armed forces were unskilled, the war exacerbated the acute shortage of skilled manpower that had been growing more severe since the mass flight of professionals, technicians, and other high-level manpower during and after the revolution: many skilled mechanics, technicians, engineers, and others were inducted into the military and the expanding military industries.

Most modern Iranian military plants were established in the 1970s by the shah, and produced a variety of small arms as well as servicing and repairing aircraft. The war with Iraq and the embargo that major industrialized countries imposed on arms shipments to both sides forced Iran to greatly expand its domestic defense industries. The government converted many of the country's most modern and well-equipped industrial plants into munitions factories,[12] and the quasi-autonomous Revolutionary Guards established military-industrial plants separate from the Defense Industries Organization.

Eventually, Iranian officials claimed to be self-sufficient in small arms, machine guns, recoilless rifles, mortars, antitank grenade launchers, ammunition, and to have test-piloted a fighter plane modeled on the American F-5.[13] Another official claimed that Iran was producing medium-range radar, pilotless aircraft, helicopters, speedboats, and cargo ships.[14] By 1989, 40,000-45,000 people were reportedly employed in various military industries producing light arms, ammunition, missiles, and aircraft parts as well as jet fighters and transport planes.[15] According to one analyst, since 1985 domestic production of military equipment has reduced Iran's annual arms imports by about $500 million.[16] Another analyst cautioned

---

[10] *New York Times* (*NYT*), January 26, 1989, p. A8.

[11] See Table 2. The figures in the text are annual averages.

[12] Robert E. Looney, *Manpower Policies and Development in the Persian Gulf Region* (Westport, CT: Praeger, 1994), p. 63.

[13] *Middle East* (April 1988), p. 18; *MEED*, February 27, 1988, p. 9.

[14] *MEED*, January 2, 1988, p. 12.

[15] Amirahmadi, pp. 146-148.

[16] Ibid., p. 146. In a 1994 study, Shahram Chubin stated that Iran produced forty-nine types of ammunition, designed and produced its own missiles and a type of tank, was developing a light passenger plane, trained its own pilots, and repaired most of its own aircraft. He cited an estimate of Iran's annual "savings" from its domestic arms industries through import substitution of $900 million to $2 billion, but then asserted that "defense industries that attempt to go beyond repair works incur high unit costs" (i.e., the cost of local production exceeds the price of imports); see Chubin, *Iran's National Security Policy*,

that lists of Iran's supposed domestically produced military products offer

> an exaggerated view of Iranian military production capabilities . . . . [P]roduction
> levels are actually quite modest. . . . Many weapons . . . are crude . . . copies of
> obsolete foreign systems [and therefore] Iran will remain dependent on foreign
> suppliers for all but a few categories of arms as well as spare parts for the
> foreseeable future.[17]

Though these claims probably were somewhat exaggerated, the arms embargo undoubtedly encouraged the development of both Iran's military industries and as one writer phrased it, "local ingenuity and the Iranian penchant for innovation."[18] The authorities have many reasons for supporting domestic defense industries—including nationalism, the need to maintain employment,[19] and fear of future arms embargoes—but in many cases, the economic basis for these industries is weak. The post-war drive to enhance Iran's conventional and unconventional military capabilities has come at the expense of the non-military industries (other than oil) and the economy as a whole.[20]

IRAN'S POST-WAR MILITARY SPENDING

According to ACDA, Iran's average annual military expenditures declined from 9.5 percent of GNP in 1986-87 to 5.8 percent in 1990-91. Similarly, its average annual arms imports dropped from $2.4 billion in 1986-88 to $1.4 billion in 1989-91.[21] Other estimates of military spending indicate an even steeper decline from over $14 billion in 1985 to $5.8 billion in 1989 and then $3.2 billion in 1990.[22] Beginning in the early 1990s, however, Iran appears to have embarked on an arms build-up. In addition to the political and strategic ramifications of the Persian Gulf War (which undoubtedly had an impact on Iran's strategic-military thinking), there was a sharp increase in oil prices in 1990-91 that enabled Iran to

---

(Washington, DC: Carnegie Endowment for International Peace, 1994), p. 19.

[17] Michael Eisenstadt, "An Assessment of Iran's Military Build-Up," in ed. Patrick Clawson, *Iran's Strategic Intentions and Capabilities* (Washington, DC: National Defense University, 1994), p. 143.

[18] Jahangir Amuzegar, *Iran's Economy under the Islamic Republic* (London: I.B. Taurus & Co., 1993), p. 299.

[19] A 1996 study estimated the number of workers employed in these plants at about 45,000, which is roughly the same figure cited in the late 1980s; see Michael Eisenstadt, *Iranian Military Power: Capabilities and Intentions*, Policy Paper no. 42 (Washington, DC: Washington Institute for Near East Policy, 1996), pp. 62-63.

[20] *Middle East Review* (1990), p. 70. These policies, unless radically altered, bode ill for Iran's economic future.

[21] See Table 2.

[22] Shahram Chubin, *Iran's National Security Policy*, pp. 34-37.

increase imports of both civilian and military equipment.[23] The first Five-Year Plan, which was adopted after Rafsanjani's election to the presidency in mid-1989, included annual allocations of $2 billion for arms imports.[24] Other sources give different estimates of Iranian arms imports in the 1990s. A report by the U.S. Congressional Research Service gives an estimate of $5.3 billion in 1990-93, of which Russia alone supplied $3.4 billion and China $1.3 billion.[25] According to Eisenstadt, annual outlays have not topped $850 million.[26]

Press reports of Iranian arms acquisitions since the early 1990s include sixty MiG-29 fighters, fifteen SU-24 fighter-bombers, and three Kilo-class submarines from Russia (the last of which was delivered in January 1997); twelve F7 fighters from China; and a consignment of SCUD missiles from North Korea.[27] Other sources assert that more weapons, including cruise missiles, are scheduled for delivery to Iran from these suppliers. According to one report, Iran concluded a "strategic agreement worth billions of dollars" with China to strengthen its armed forces.[28] There are also reported deals with Russia for a large number of T-72 tanks as well as bombers and other aircraft.[29] In 1995, a Polish official stated that Warsaw had agreed to sell Iran over 100 T-72 tanks.[30]

In an apparent response to U.S. criticism that Iran had embarked on a massive rearmament program and intended to develop weapons of mass destruction (including nuclear bombs), the Iranian defense minister asserted in 1993 that Iran does not regard the very large weapons orders by Saudi Arabia and other Gulf countries since the 1991 Gulf War as a threat "to its friendly relations with its neighboring countries."[31] Iran "has no intention" of being "dragged into . . . an arms race," he said, and will focus instead on "economic reconstruction," adding that Iran's defense spending "is a mere 3.8 percent of its GNP," that 50 percent of Iranian military industries' production is civilian goods, and that the armed forces are similarly utilized in scores of civilian reconstruction projects.[32]

The United States and Iran's neighbors have a different view. In early 1992, the U.S. director of central intelligence told a U.S. Senate committee that "Iran has embarked on an across-the-board effort to develop its military and defense industries [including] weapons of mass destruction,

---

[23] See Tables 2 and 5.

[24] Chubin, *Iran's National Security Policy*, p. 34.

[25] Richard F. Grimmett, *Conventional Arms Transfers to Developing Nations: 1987-94*, CRS Report No. 95-862-F (Washington, DC: Congressional Research Service, August 4, 1995).

[26] Eisenstadt, "An Assessment of Iran's Military Build-Up," p. 100.

[27] Economist Intelligence Unit (EIU), *Country Profile–Iran* (1995-96), p. 11.

[28] Yossef Bodansky, "The Grand Strategy of Iran," *Global Affairs* 8, no. 4 (1993), pp. 30-32.

[29] *Middle East* (January 1994), p. 17.

[30] *NYT*, May 17,1995, p. A5.

[31] *MEED*, April 30, 1993, p. 19.

[32] Ibid.

. . . [and] continues to shop in Western markets for nuclear and missile technology."[33] Secretary of State Warren Christopher described Iran as an "international outlaw" and expressed concern that North Korea was selling new intermediate-range (1,000 km) ballistic missiles to Iran.[34] In apparent rebuttal, Iran's minister of defense stated that his country's limited defense budget allocated only $850 million in foreign exchange to arms imports in fiscal 1993-94, was developing its own defense industries, and therefore had no need to purchase new weapons.[35] All sources indicate a significant slowdown in Iranian arms imports since 1992-93, even if their absolute figures differ. The critical shortage of foreign exchange and rapid growth of foreign debt reportedly forced Iran to cancel more than $5 billion in arms deals in 1993 alone, including a contract for a MiG-29 assembly line.[36] That same year, the Central Bank governor urged the government to reduce military and other imports.[37]

At the same time, however, nuclear experts from Russia and China reportedly arrived in Tehran to work on its nuclear programs. Russia was reportedly selling two 440-MW power reactors and China was supplying two similar reactors as well as two research reactors. U.S. intelligence sources claimed that Iran was continuing to shop for weapons-related nuclear equipment and expertise, concentrating on the former Soviet republics.[38] In 1995, Russia reportedly agreed to complete construction of a nuclear plant started by two German companies in 1974 but abandoned after the revolution and subsequently heavily damaged during the war with Iraq. The agreement with Russia calls for the completion of the 1,000 MW nuclear reactor within four years at a cost of $800 million.[39]

The head of Iran's Atomic Energy Organization stated that its efforts were purely civilian. The goal, he said, was to provide 20 percent of Iran's electricity needs through nuclear power by the year 2000. The leaders of the revolution had criticized a similar program under the shah to develop nuclear-powered electricity (as well as nuclear weapons) as wasteful for a country rich in oil and gas resources,[40] and on purely economic grounds they were probably right. Moreover, since 1993 the economic constraints have become more severe, due primarily to the decline in oil revenues. For these reasons, the United States and others view Iran's assurances that its nuclear program is benign with a healthy skepticism.

---

[33] *Middle East* (April 1993), p. 36.

[34] *MEED*, April 23, 1993, pp. 22-23.

[35] Ibid., March 12, 1993, p. 10.

[36] Eisenstadt, "An Assessment of Iran's Military Build-Up," p. 100.

[37] *MEED*, April 30, 1993, pp. 2-3.

[38] *Wall Street Journal* (*WSJ*), May 11, 1993, p. A14.

[39] *NYT*, January 9, 1995, p. 4; *MEED*, January 20, 1995, p. 21.

[40] *MEED*, April 30, 1993, p. 19; *NYT*, May 19, 1995, p. 1.

VII

Labor, Employment, and Income

Since the 1980s, Iran has had a high level of hidden or disguised unemployment, especially in public sector enterprises and the civil service.[1] In addition, the decline in real wages during this period induced or compelled many civil servants and others to take second jobs (e.g., as taxi drivers or cigarette vendors) which are ignored or understated in the census and other official statistics. This "informal employment" has taken on much larger dimensions since the 1980s, but reasonably accurate data on its magnitude, wages, and personal incomes are sparse and (when available) often of doubtful validity—in part because of tax avoidance. Official estimates of personal consumption (assuming they are reasonably accurate) can serve as a "proxy" for changes in income because—at least over the long term—income and consumption are closely correlated.

LABOR DISTRIBUTION BY SECTOR

Employment data for industry—broadly defined to include the oil sector, manufacturing, mining, construction, and public utilities—show an overall decline during the Iran-Iraq War and then an increase between 1986 and 1990. Industry's share of total employment, which was as high as 37 percent in 1976, declined sharply to 17 percent in 1990. The magnitude of the decline is hardly credible, however, particularly in view of widely reported hidden unemployment in public sector industries.[2] For many years, employment in large manufacturing establishments (those employing ten or more workers), which account for an important share of the industrial sector, increased more rapidly than production yet hardly decreased (and in some cases actually *increased*) during periods of declining production. This implies flat or declining labor productivity.

According to official estimates, employment in the service sector—broadly defined to include health, education, various professional and

---

[1] Employment data in most developing countries are not very reliable, and Iran is no exception. There are often wide gaps between official Iranian estimates of unemployment, higher estimates by various government ministers, and still higher unofficial estimates.

[2] Hooshang Amirahmadi, *Revolution and Economic Transition: The Iranian Experience* (Albany, NY: State University of New York Press, 1990), p. 191; Economist Intelligence Unit (EIU), *Country Profile–Iran* (1995-96), p. 21. The figure quoted by the EIU for 1986 employment in industry is much lower than that quoted in Amirahmadi. See also Robert Looney, *Manpower Policies and Development in the Persian Gulf Region* (Westport, CT: Praeger, 1994), pp. 63-70.

personal services, government bureaucrats, finance, trade and commerce, transportation, and communications—accounted for about 35 percent of total employment from 1976 to 1984, increased to 42 percent in 1986, and thence to 46 percent (5.6 million workers) in 1990.[3] The so-called "informal sector"—the black market trade in foreign currency, smuggled cigarettes, and government ration coupons—which should be included in this category, has also grown very rapidly. Tehran University economist Hamid Ansari estimated that the number of people engaged in these and similar (mostly illicit) activities had increased sharply from about 1 million before the revolution to some 3.5 million in 1990-91.[4] For obvious reasons, most of this informal economic activity goes unreported.

If these estimates are assumed to be reasonably accurate and are added to formal employment figures, far more than half of total employment (excluding the armed forces) in the early 1990s was in the service sector. According to one calculation, nine out of ten new jobs created in the decade after the revolution were in services. More than 2.3 million new jobs created since the revolution were in the broadly defined public sector, mostly in services.[5] In the early 1990s, there were an estimated 2 million government employees (not including state-owned enterprises), compared to 800,000 in 1977. According to Iran's Organization for Employment Affairs, the "productive labor of each government employee is less than one hour per day"—in other words, the majority were redundant.[6]

According to estimates from the U.S. Department of Agriculture, agriculture's share of total Iranian employment has been steadily declining from about 40 percent before the Islamic revolution to about 28 percent in 1992.[7] Official Iranian estimates of agriculture's share of total employment are 29.2 percent in 1986 and 27.6 percent in 1990. In absolute terms, however, there was a small increase in agricultural employment.[8]

EMPLOYMENT AND UNEMPLOYMENT

The oil boom of the 1970s resulted in labor shortages that led to the employment of 1 million Afghans in Iran, mainly in agriculture and other unskilled manual labor, and enticed many Iranians working abroad to return home. The Islamic revolution and war with Iraq reversed this situation. An estimated 2-4 million Iranians—mostly engineers, managers,

---

[3] EIU, *Country Profile–Iran* (1995-96), p. 21; Amirahmadi, p. 191. Presumably for national security reasons, the size of the armed forces is often omitted from the service sector.

[4] In many cases, they are civil servants seeking to supplement meager salaries; see *Economist,* May 11, 1991, p. 38; Amirahmadi, p. 191.

[5] Jahangir Amuzegar, *Iran's Economy under the Islamic Republic* (London: I.B. Taurus & Co., 1993), p. 59-64.

[6] *Middle East Report* (November-December 1994), p. 21.

[7] See Table 11.

[8] EIU, *Country Profile–Iran* (1995-96), p. 21.

skilled technicians, and other professionals needed to develop the economy—fled the country during and after the revolution. Their absence was one of the primary causes for Iran's poor economic performance and consequent rising unemployment thereafter.[9] In addition, about 3 million Afghans who fled their country in the wake of the 1979 Soviet invasion sought refuge in Iran.[10] Similarly, Iran provided safehaven to about 500,000 Iraqi Kurds and Shi'a during the Iran-Iraq War (and again during and after the 1990-91 Persian Gulf War). For the most part, the absorption of these refugees aggravated Iran's unemployment problems.[11]

Thus, despite large-scale mobilization by the armed forces and the expansion of military industries during the war, according to official estimates unemployment actually *increased* from 10.5 percent in 1977 to 11.7 percent in 1980 and 15.9 percent in 1988 due to the stagnant or declining economy,[12] before declining again to 9 percent in 1994 as the economy began to recover in the early 1990s. Non-official estimates, however, put unemployment as high as 29 percent in 1986. One Iranian official was quoted as saying that the unemployment rate in 1989 was 24 percent,[13] and Amuzegar estimated that overt unemployment remained around 25 percent in 1993-94.[14] Those figures did not take into account "hidden" unemployment—jobs created for political and social rather than economic reasons and disguised by deliberate overstaffing in public and private sector employment—and the phenomenal growth of the informal sector. A British economic journal notes that

> large areas of disguised unemployment persist in all sectors. Farming activity is mainly confined to the warm months of the year and [public sector] industry retains many workers in employment for welfare purposes. The services category covers a large number of people who are underemployed, engaged in activities such as selling cigarettes.[15]

Some observers suggest that the problem stems in part from the fact that many of the unemployed (particularly university graduates) will not accept manual labor jobs in agriculture, construction, or industry, which are most often done by Afghans and uneducated Iranians, and insist instead on "white collar" positions.[16] Reducing the high rate of unemployment and

---

[9] Ibid. (1985-86), pp. 13-22; *Economist*, May 2, 1991, p. 51. According to one estimate, the exodus included half of Iran's physicians; see Shahram Chubin and Charles Tripp, *Iran and Iraq at War* (Boulder, CO: Westview Press, 1988), p. 131.

[10] Though many Afghans returned home after Soviet forces withdrew, an estimated 500,000 were still in Iran in 1995; see *Economist*, July 1, 1995, p. 33.

[11] *Financial Times (FT)*, April 12, 1991, p. 4.

[12] Unofficial estimates were even higher; see Table 8.

[13] Amirahmadi, p. 187; see also Table 8, note 1.

[14] *Wall Street Journal (WSJ)*, January 3, 1994, p. 8.

[15] EIU, *Country Profile–Iran* (1995-96), p. 21.

[16] *Middle East* (November 1988), pp. 23-24.

the potential danger it poses to political and social stability will require several years of significant, sustained economic growth.

EDUCATION AND LABOR QUALITY

In addition to capital resources, economic development requires high-quality labor—broadly defined as skilled workers, technicians, managers, and other professionals. There is considerable evidence that the overall quality of the Iranian labor force has deteriorated since the revolution. Iran's total spending on education, as a percentage of GNP, is lower than that of many other developing countries, most of which do not have the benefit of large oil revenues. In 1991-92, 1.8 million children (out of a total of 12 million) were reportedly unable to attend school because of a lack of facilities. There is a high drop-out rate from high schools. Despite Iran's desperate need for technicians and its large agriculture sector, among high school students only 15 percent are enrolled in vocational programs and less than 1 percent in agricultural schools.[17]

The quality of university education has clearly declined. Many faculty fled the country before and after the revolution and were difficult to replace.[18] After coming to power, the clerical regime closed Iran's universities for several years under the slogan of "Cultural Revolution" and the "Islamization" of education. They purged some of the remaining faculty and made sure the curricula did not conflict with the ideas of the revolution and Islam. According to one observer of Iran's medical schools,

> The wave of purges following the Islamization program left the universities almost deserted [of qualified staff]. Those who left were, on the whole, younger and more skilled. New programs of medical education introduced by the revolution mean that new graduates will be less qualified than the previous ones.[19]

When the doors reopened in 1982, the number of students admitted was sharply reduced from 175,000 in 1978-79 to 117,000 in 1982.[20] Though these numbers have since increased, nearly half of the university openings are "reserved for politically endorsed candidates who are not required to take the standard entrance examination."[21] To make matters worse, jobs

---

[17] Amuzegar, p. 64.

[18] Amirahmadi, pp. 90, 189.

[19] M. Malek, "The Impact of Iran's Islamic Revolution on Health Personnel Policy," *World Development* 19, no. 8 (August 1991), pp. 1045-54. According to one estimate, roughly half of all physicians fled Iran before and after the revolution; see Chubin and Tripp, p. 131.

[20] See Table 8.

[21] Amuzegar, p. 64. This is similar to the policy of selecting senior personnel in government and state-owned industries from those considered "Islamically correct"; see *WSJ*, May 11, 1995, pp. A1, A13. Lower educational and managerial standards have a negative impact on economic performance and retard Iran's development.

available to graduates of even the best universities offer meager salaries.[22] A 1988 report estimated that only about 15 percent of Iranians who go abroad to pursue or continue their university studies return to Iran.[23]

In the early 1990s, the authorities began taking limited steps to address the shortage of critical personnel—by creating so-called "pockets of excellence" in some industrial plants,[24] for example—but the results have been meager in relation to the country's needs. According to a British economic journal, "[t]here is a deep sense of unease that the failure of the educational and training system over the last decade has left the country without adequate managers and technicians, especially given that the 'brain drain' occurring since the 1979 revolution has left the country deprived of its trained elite."[25]

INCOME DIFFERENTIALS AND LIVING STANDARDS

According to the data for 1970-85, real (i.e., inflation-adjusted) wages rose by an annual average of 15.6 percent during 1970-77—an unusually rapid rate of growth even during a boom. But more incredible is the even higher 21 percent annual growth rate during 1977-80, a period of severe economic problems, rising unemployment, and declining living standards. This was followed by a decline of 13 percent during 1980-85. According to these figures, real wages in 1985 (the depth of a serious recession) were 54 percent *higher* than in 1977 (the peak year of the pre-revolution boom).[26]

In the absence of reliable data on wages (or other components of personal income), estimates of living standards—defined as real private consumption *per capita*—can be used to measure changes in income because the two are closely related. During 1970-77, living standards rose 10.7 percent annually compared to a 7.6 percent annual increase in *per capita* GDP. During the 1977-80 recession, the former fell 8 percent annually and the latter about twice that. During 1980-85 (a period of moderate recovery), both indices rose a scant 1 percent annually, and during 1985-88 they both fell by about 10-11 percent annually. During the 1988-91 post-war recovery, however, living standards rose more than 11 percent annually—roughly double the rate of growth of real GDP *per capita*. During 1991-94, living standards fell while *per capita* GDP rose by less than 1 percent annually. Given that *per capita* GDP declined 50 percent during 1977-94, living standards probably fell by more than the 20 percent

---

[22] *New York Times* (*NYT*), July 23, 1990, p. A2.

[23] *FT*, November 23, 1988, p. 24.

[24] *Middle East Economic Digest* (*MEED*), February 24, 1995, p. 2.

[25] EIU, *Country Report–Iran*, no. 1 (1991), p. 14.

[26] This may be the reason that the International Monetary Fund (IMF) discontinued this series of reports after 1985; see IMF, *International Financial Statistics Yearbook*, vol. 47 (Washington, DC: IMF, 1994), pp. 422-23.

indicated in the official data for the same period.[27] Even if the gap between the two indicators was narrower, the data are consistent with the thesis that households resist sharp reductions in their living standards during periods of declining incomes by utilizing accumulated savings or other means.

These figures represent broad national averages, however; incomes rose more rapidly for the wealthy elite than most of the population during 1970-77, causing the income differential (the gap between rich and poor) to widen considerably and adding impetus to the revolution.[28] The reforms instituted in the early years of the revolution to help the poor—such as nationalization of various enterprises, land reform, and the establishment of the *bonyads*—led to a short-term narrowing of income differentials during 1979-80.[29] After 1981, however, this trend reversed. Based on income levels reported in the 1986 census, a member of parliament estimated that 25 percent of Iran's population were "very deprived," 47 percent were "vulnerable," 25 percent were "semi-vulnerable," and 3 percent were affluent. He concluded that "post-revolution Iran has increasingly become polarized into a two-class society of the rich and the poor," with the rich constituting only a small fraction of the population.[30]

According to an independent 1989 study of official data, rising unemployment among the urban poor increased the number of households living in poverty and further expanded income inequality.[31] This conclusion was confirmed by a 1989 Ministry of Finance estimate, which found that the poorest 40 percent of the population earned only 2.9 percent of national income, the middle 40 percent earned 22.1 percent, and the top 20 percent earned 75 percent.[32] A 1993 study reported estimates that about 60 percent of the population was living below the "poverty line" (defined as a monthly income equivalent to $158), and noted that "Iranian society is seen as being polarized into two classes, the very rich and the very poor."[33] A 1990 *Financial Times* report quoted a Tehran journal's warning that poverty could "impede the progress of the revolution and, if unattended, eventually destroy it."[34] Two years later, the *Times* said that "[t]he poor are becoming poorer, and the middle class, with the exception of the privileged few, is being squeezed by soaring prices—few can survive without working two or even three jobs."[35]

---

[27] The wide gap between the two may be due in part to the underestimation of inflation in the official consumer price index; see Table 12.

[28] EIU, *Country Profile–Iran* (1991-92), p. 21.

[29] Amirahmadi, p. 202.

[30] Ibid.

[31] Sohrab Behdad, "Winners and Losers of the Iranian Revolution: A Study of Income Distribution," *International Journal of Middle East Studies* (August 1989), pp. 327-58.

[32] *Middle East* (September 1989), pp. 29-30.

[33] Amuzegar, p. 291.

[34] *FT*, March 6, 1990, p. 4.

[35] Ibid., June 12, 1992, p. 4.

VIII

Economic Planning, Foreign Trade, and External Debt

Oil export revenues remain Iran's primary means of earning the foreign exchange it needs to finance imports of the machinery, raw materials, and spare parts required for investment and production. Economic growth is usually measured by changes in GDP adjusted for inflation. During 1970-77, Iran's real average annual GDP growth was 10.6 percent (7.6 percent *per capita*), due primarily to the impact of burgeoning oil revenues.[1] Non-oil GDP expanded at an even more rapid annual rate of 12.6 percent (9.5 percent *per capita*). Investment (gross fixed capital formation) was the driving force behind this growth, rising 21 percent annually during 1970-77.[2] According to official figures, oil export revenues reached a peak of 86 percent of total budget revenues in 1974, and then dropped to 74 percent in 1977. In 1986, however, oil prices were at their lowest and oil revenues fell to only 25 percent of total revenues.

NON-OIL EXPORTS

In the 1970s and 1980s, oil accounted for about 95 percent of total merchandise exports. Due to the volatility and unreliability of oil prices, however, the government's goal is to reduce dependence on oil revenues by developing other sectors of the economy. Moreover, the oil industry is highly capital-intensive (i.e., employs few people) and therefore raising non-oil GDP enhances job creation. Thus, the growth of Iran's non-oil GDP is an important measure of its economic progress (or lack thereof). Iran's traditional non-oil exports have been carpets, fruit, leather, caviar, and other agricultural products. During the 1974-78 oil boom, non-oil exports (most of which come from the private sector) generally stagnated at an annual level of $500-600 million. They declined to an annual average of $360 million during 1981-85, due partly to production bottlenecks arising from import restrictions on raw materials, spare parts, and other inputs. Cotton exports almost ceased in the 1980s as a result of the instability prevailing in the main growing areas during the war with Iraq.

---

[1] With annual population growth averaging 2.7 percent in the last decade, it is also important to measure economic growth on a *per capita* basis; see Table 3.

[2] See Table 12.

The widening gap between the official and the much higher black market exchange rates encouraged widespread smuggling of goods *out* of Iran. One official estimated that in 1985 illegal exports equaled the $465 million in legal exports.[3] When the government subsequently changed its policies and offered exporters a much higher exchange rate and other incentives, legal non-oil exports rose rapidly from about $1 billion annually during 1986-89 to $4.5 billion in 1994.[4] Carpet exports, which had declined sharply through most of the 1980s, rose strongly from $115 million in 1985 to $1.4 billion in 1993 and $1.6 billion in 1994, when they accounted for 37 percent of total non-oil exports. Agricultural goods and traditional handicrafts such as carpets accounted for two-thirds of Iranian non-oil exports in 1994, with the balance being mostly refined copper, metal ores, chemicals, and textiles.[5] Although much of this increase is believed to have been diverted from the black to the legal market, there are indications that large-scale smuggling continued.[6] Until Iran can increase its non-oil exports to many multiples of their current level, however, it will remain dependent on oil revenues to finance development and much of its public and private consumption.

PLANNING AND INVESTMENT

The 1973-78 Five-Year Development Plan, adopted shortly before the first international oil crisis, was outdated before the ink was dry. As soaring oil prices increased revenues, Iran's investment doubled to $70 billion and military expenditures rose very sharply—far beyond the levels stipulated in the plan. Public investment in infrastructure included roads, railways, air- and seaports, communications, dams, irrigation, reservoirs, electric power, education, and healthcare facilities. In addition, the government invested in industries requiring large amounts of capital, which the private sector was unable or unwilling to supply. In some cases, this took the form of joint ventures with domestic or foreign private investors. Though smaller in absolute terms, private investment grew more rapidly and concentrated primarily in housing, light industry, trade, and commerce.

The rapid increase in both public and private investment and consumption overheated the economy and (along with labor shortages) stoked inflationary pressures. The consumer price index, which had increased by a mere 2 percent in 1970, rose by an annual average of 12 percent during 1973-76, before more than doubling to 28 percent in

---

[3] Clawson, "Islamic Iran's Economic Politics and Prospects," *Middle East Journal* (summer 1988), p. 384.

[4] Ibid.

[5] Economist Intelligence Unit (EIU), *Country Profile–Iran* (1995-96), p. 44.

[6] *Iran Focus* (September 1990), p. 12. A sharp policy reversal in 1995 requiring exporters to accept a significantly lower exchange rate has led to the resumption of "underinvoicing" and illegal exports; see *Financial Times (FT)*, May 24, 1995, p. 6.

1977.[7] Despite the much higher rate of inflation, however, living standards (real private consumption *per capita*) rose by an annual rate of 10.7 percent during 1970-77.[8] But growing inflation and the widening gap between the rich and the poor fueled rising discontent and eventually sparked the Islamic revolution.

The turmoil of the revolution had particularly adverse effects on government investment. Capital expenditures fell from 14 percent of GDP in 1974-78 to 8 percent in 1980-83. Although increasing investment—particularly in infrastructure—was imperative to developing the economy, political exigencies and the war with Iraq gave priority to current expenditures. Measured in constant prices, public investment fell nearly every year during 1978-88 to less than 25 percent of 1977 public sector investment. Though it subsequently doubled between 1988 and 1992, this figure was still less than half that of 1977.[9]

By 1987-88, total public and private investment was down to half the levels in 1983-84. After deducting capital consumption allowances,[10] net investment was not much above zero and may actually have been negative (even without taking into account war damage). The effect of these policies was to reduce the productive base of the economy. Infrastructure such as ports, bridges, and power stations suffered from neglect as well as Iraqi bombing. Power shortages became common, inconveniencing households and seriously damaging industry and other economic sectors.

After the war, parliament and newly elected president Rafsanjani formally adopted the 1989-93 Five-Year Development Plan, which set average annual growth rate targets of 8.2 percent for GDP, 9.6 percent for oil, 6.1 percent for agriculture, 14 percent for industry, and 6-7 percent for various services. Revenues from exports of oil (and a small amount of natural gas) were projected at $83 billion over the five-year period. The planners based this on the expectation that oil exports would grow from 1.5 MBD in 1988 to 2.3 MBD in 1993, and that oil prices would rise over the five-year period from $14.2 to $21.4 per barrel. They also projected that non-oil exports would total $17.8 billion over the five-year period.

To achieve these goals, annual investment was targeted to rise by 12 percent. Imports were projected at $114 billion, including $9.5 billion for "defense and security."[11] Though government officials assumed that GDP would rise faster than public and private consumption, they recognized that export earnings and national savings would be insufficient to finance planned investment and growth in imports, which would require recourse

---

[7] See Table 3; EIU, *Country Profile–Iran* (1991-92), p. 17.

[8] See Table 12.

[9] See Tables 7 and 10.

[10] Capital consumption allowances are generally estimates of depreciation of capital stock. The damage and destruction caused by the war added to normal depreciation in Iran.

[11] EIU, *Country Profile–Iran* (1991-92), pp. 17-18; Hooshang Amirahmadi, *Revolution and Economic Transition: The Iranian Experience* (Albany, NY: State University of New York Press, 1990), pp. 252-56; *MidEast Markets*, September 18, 1989, p. 4.

to unprecedented (for Iran) external borrowing and foreign private investment, estimated at almost $18 billion over five years—greatly exceeding the provisions for external finance in the development plan.[12]

In 1991, Rafsanjani and his oil minister projected that oil production would rise to 3.9 MBD by the end of the year, reach 4.5 MBD the following year, and 5 MBD in 1993.[13] In fact, output rose far less than that, from 3.4 MBD in 1991 to 3.7 MBD in 1992, and then fell slightly to 3.6 MBD in 1993 (where it remained in 1994 and the first half of 1995).[14] The failure to even come close to the announced goals and virtual stagnancy of oil output in the early 1990s was due to financial and technical constraints, not quotas set by OPEC.[15] Similarly, the 1989-93 Five-Year Plan's various growth rate targets—and the rates actually achieved—are shown below.

Average Annual Growth Rates and Total Revenues, 1990-94[16]

	Target	Actual
Gross Domestic Product (GDP)	8.2 percent	6.3 percent
Agriculture	6.1 percent	6.1 percent
Oil	9.6 percent	5.7 percent
Industry	14.3 percent	8.5 percent
Investment	12 percent	12.6 percent
Private consumption	5.8 percent	7.8 percent
Public consumption	3.8 percent	10.4 percent
Total oil export revenues (1990-94)	$83.0 billion	$79.8 billion
Total non-oil export revenues (1990-94)	$17.8 billion	$15.1 billion

The failure to achieve the targets for GDP, oil, and industry was serious, particularly in view of the considerable unused industrial capacity. More important than the low growth rates for various sectors, however, was the overall trend for the economy as a whole. A closer examination of sectoral data indicates that growth rates were favorable during the immediate post-war period (1988-91), but that economic indicators began to slow down by 1992 and were mostly unfavorable in the subsequent two years.[17] In 1993 and 1994, *per capita* growth rates for industry and GDP were either flat or negative. The annual growth in investment, which had been

---

[12] Because many parliamentarians were ideologically opposed to foreign loans and investment, annual budget deficits (which fell from 4 percent of GDP in 1989 to less than 2 percent in 1992) were financed largely by borrowing from the Central Bank.

[13] *Gulf States Newsletter,* December 16, 1991, pp. 6, 11; *Middle East Economic Digest (MEED),* December 27, 1991, p. 10.

[14] *Petroleum Economist* (October 1995), p. 60.

[15] OPEC is the Organization of Petroleum Exporting Countries. Historically, Iran has paid little attention to OPEC quotas and has expanded production capacity whenever possible to increase output; considering its economic condition, it could hardly afford to do otherwise.

[16] For a variety of reasons, implementation of the 1989-93 plan was postponed until 1990; see EIU, *Country Profile–Iran* (1991-92), pp. 17-18.

[17] See Table 12.

19 percent during 1988-91, dropped to 7 percent in 1992 and 3 percent in 1993-94.

Private consumption, however, rose considerably more than projected over the five-year span, and public consumption climbed even more rapidly. There were calls for wage increases for civil servants (whose salaries had been severely eroded by inflation)[18] and greater subsidies for producers and consumers, and other demands on the treasury. At the same time, tax collections as a percentage of GDP dropped from 5.6 percent in 1991-92 to somewhat over 4 percent in 1993-94.

With total consumption having risen faster than the growth rate of the economy, Iranian officials faced an unpleasant choice: either increase external financing or curtail investment with all its negative effects on economic growth, employment, and incomes. Ultimately, they chose both: annual growth in investment slowed to about 3 percent in 1993-94, and external borrowing expanded greatly until 1992-93, when for the first time Iran was unable to make payments and in effect defaulted on its debt.

In 1994, the government adopted the 1995-99 Five-Year Plan. Though few details of the plan are available, it reportedly envisages a 27 percent increase in total expenditures in this period.[19] Half of the revenues are to be derived from oil exports, one-quarter from taxes,[20] and the rest from "other sources." The plan foresees oil production (3.6 MBD in 1994) increasing to 4.5 MBD by the end of the decade. Petrochemicals are projected to expand by 50 percent, much of it for export. In addition, priority is given to expanding agro-industries, mining, and other non-oil exports, which are projected to rise by 8.5 percent annually.

Overall, the plan aims for a modest annual economic growth of 5.1 percent over five years. The main objective is to increase employment by some 2 million jobs over that period.[21] One of the other major goals is to

---

[18] The official estimate of inflation in 1994 was 35 percent, but unofficial estimates ranged from 50 to 100 percent—while salaries remained constant; see *New York Times* (*NYT*), May 20, 1995, pp. A1, A8.

[19] By contrast, the announced budgets for fiscal 1994-95 and 1995-96 indicated sharp cuts in government spending when adjusted for rial inflation. As one economic journal noted, however, Iran's "published budgets [often] bear little resemblance to actual expenditure and revenue at the end of the year because of the government's persistently optimistic view of potential oil income and underestimation of expenditures." See EIU, *Country Report–Iran*, no. 2 (1994), p. 16; and *Country Profile–Iran* (1995-96), p. 41.

[20] Relatively low government tax revenues (5-6 percent of GDP) reflect not only the relatively large contribution of oil to total revenues but also massive tax evasion. In 1987, Prime Minister Mousavi spoke of "unpaid taxes on the astronomical profits made under war conditions," mainly by merchants; see Amirahmadi, p. 170. In 1988, the deputy prime minister suggested that only one-third of taxes due were actually being collected; see *MEED*, August 12, 1988, pp. 8, 11. The following year, the finance minister was somewhat more conservative, suggesting that evasion amounted to "only" half of taxes due; see *MidEast Markets*, April 3, 1989, p. 5. Excise taxes on cigarettes, beverages, cars, and other goods fluctuate but generally contribute a very small share of total revenues.

[21] In addition, agricultural production is to rise by 4.5 percent and industry and mining by 5.9 percent annually.

reduce the annual rate of inflation from 20-35 percent in 1991-94 to an annual average of 12.5 percent in the second half of the decade, although higher rates of economic growth are likely to accelerate rather than moderate inflation.[22] Whether Iran achieves these relatively modest goals will depend on many factors, particularly its ability to implement economically effective but politically destabilizing policies. Until that is done, the volume of oil production and exports will remain of cardinal importance. Unless Iran considerably increases foreign participation in the development of its oil (and gas) resources, the magnitude of its revenues will continue to depend largely on world oil prices.

GOVERNMENT EXPENDITURES

Under the shah, total government expenditures rose from 29 percent of GDP in 1970-73 to 44 percent in 1974-78. So-called "current" expenditures (mostly wages, salaries, and subsidies) rose from 18 to 30 percent of GDP during those intervals, while capital spending rose far more slowly from 11 to 14 percent of GDP. Measured in constant prices, public sector investment rose very strongly during 1970-77, but the fastest growing component of current expenditures was military spending, which rose from less than 8 percent of GDP in 1970 to over 15 percent in 1978.[23]

The Islamic regime initially cut back sharply on military spending and investment projects initiated under the shah. Total expenditures fell almost annually from 43 percent of GDP in 1978 to 16 percent in 1988. During 1989-92, GDP rose by a very high annual average of 9.6 percent and government spending (particularly capital expenditures) rose even more rapidly.[24] The destruction of much of Iraq's war machine in the 1991 Persian Gulf War allowed Iran to cut back on military spending,[25] while the surge in oil prices caused by the war allowed the authorities to increase spending on reconstruction and development. Imports soared to $25.2 billion in 1990-91, almost double their level in 1989, and then retreated marginally in 1992.[26] By 1993, total public expenditures were 22 percent of GDP, which was still only half of the pre-revolution level.[27] This reduction resulted from the sharp drop in public investment, a degree of wage restraint, and a transfer of many public services to the *bonyads.*[28]

---

[22] EIU, *Country Profile–Iran* (1995-96), pp. 18-19. According to one observer, high inflation has forced low-income families "to sell their durable holdings such as carpets and jewelry as a means of meeting their most fundamental requirements"; see Amirahmadi, pp. 170-202.

[23] See Tables 2 and 7. Although the U.S. Arms Control and Disarmament Agency estimates military spending in terms of GNP, there is little difference between Iran's GNP and GDP.

[24] See Tables 7 and 9.

[25] See Table 2.

[26] See Table 5.

[27] See Table 7.

[28] Jahangir Amuzegar, *Iran's Economy Under the Islamic Republic* (London: I.B. Taurus & Co.,

In addition to figures in published budgets, it is generally believed that there was substantial "off budget" (i.e., unaccounted for) spending on the military (during and since the war with Iraq);[29] indirect subsidies on oil products,[30] essential foods and medicines, and non-essential goods such as cars; loans to various public sector enterprises at negative real rates of interest; and foreign currency allocations at exchange rates below free market value.[31] Similarly, though some of the profits of the *bonyads* are used to deliver certain social services that under the shah were provided by the government, their spending is not included in the national budget.[32] In fact, none of the budgets of public sector enterprises, local governments, and various official agencies—except for the transfer of funds between these entities and the national treasury—is included in the published state budget.

MULTIPLE EXCHANGE RATES

Another major source of economic distortions is the system of multiple exchange rates that proliferated in the 1980s. Until the revolution, there was effectively only one exchange rate for all international transactions. After the revolution, this policy was abandoned and a system of multiple exchange rates evolved. The so-called "official" exchange rate was tied to the IMF's Special Drawing Rights (SDR) unit of account and fluctuated between 65 and 91 rials to the dollar.[33] By 1985, the free market rate was seven times the "official" rate,[34] and three years later this ratio had increased to fifteen to twenty times.[35]

1993), p. 96.

[29] Other military spending is hidden in a general category listed as "other expenditures."

[30] Heavily subsidized gasoline, for example, benefits mostly the upper classes, because few others can afford to own cars. A 1993 estimate by Iran's Plan and Budget Organization indicated that Tehran was spending $11 billion annually on oil subsidies, compared to oil export earnings that year of $14.3 billion; see *Middle East Economic Survey (MEES),* June 7, 1993, p. A1. One source calculated the domestic price of gasoline at eleven cents a gallon, a level probably unmatched even in the richest Arab oil states; see *Petroleum Intelligence Weekly,* July 12, 1993, p. 5. The result has been a rapid growth in domestic oil consumption from 778,000 barrels per day in 1988 to 1.2 MBD in 1995. The Majlis initially resisted Rafsanjani's attempts to reduce the gas subsidy; see *Economist,* July 16, 1994, pp. 45-46. When it later doubled the price (still far below international prices) in 1994, consumption fell slightly; see *MEED,* July 21, 1995, p. 9.

[31] It is plausible, however, that the figures in published budgets reflect general trends in public civilian expenditures.

[32] Amuzegar, p. 100. By the early 1990s, their combined budgets were equivalent to almost half of the state budget.

[33] See International Monetary Fund (IMF), *International Financial Statistics Yearbook,* vol. 47 (Washington, DC: IMF, 1994), pp. 424, 425.

[34] *Economist,* September 21, 1985, p. 52.

[35] *Middle East Review,* 1990, p. 69.

By the late 1980s, there were as many as eight legal exchange rates that applied to various categories of import and export transactions, in addition to the free (or "black") market rate. The basic "official" rate of 70 rials to the dollar applied to oil and gas exports, most imports, and some other transactions. A "preferential rate" of 420 rials to the dollar applied to some categories of imports, a "competitive" rate of 800 rials to the dollar to others, and two "incentive" rates to non-oil exports.

The policy of the IMF is to pressure countries to abandon multiple exchange rate systems, which create almost insurmountable political and social obstacles to economic reform, in favor of a realistic uniform exchange rate. But few countries have had such a wide gap between the official and free market rates. In response to IMF pressure, in January 1991 the Iranian government reduced the number of official exchange rates to "only" three: 70 rials to the dollar for oil exports, basic foods and other essential consumer imports, and military-related acquisitions; a so-called "competitive" rate of 600-800 rials to the dollar for most other imports, including raw materials, spare parts, machinery, and equipment; and a "floating" exchange rate of about 1,350 rials to the dollar—which approximated the free market rate—that applied to all other transactions.

Though this new system—effectively a partial devaluation of the currency—was an improvement over the previous system, the factor of twenty between the lowest and highest exchange rates has few if any parallels and led to severe economic distortions. Oil export revenues, for example, continued to be recorded in the national budget at the absurdly low official rate, thereby understating their real contribution to the budget and the economy. Measured in dollars, annual oil export revenues rose sharply from $12 billion in 1989 to $17.9 billion in 1990, and then fell back slightly to $16-17 billion in 1991 and 1992. Official accounts for this period, however, indicate a *decline* of oil receipts.[36] This undervaluation increased as high inflation continued to erode the real value of the rial.[37]

In November 1991, the governor of the Central Bank stated that the government was committed to instituting a uniform exchange rate no later than March 1994.[38] Although a single market-related rate (essentially another major devaluation of the rial) would greatly reduce opportunities for corruption and improve economic performance in the long term, its immediate effect would almost certainly be inflationary—much higher prices for food and other essential goods. Moreover, according to a 1992 study, it would force "about 80 percent of manufacturing [enterprises to]

---

[36] Similarly, government imports of food and other "essential" goods were recorded at the lowest official exchange rate, grossly understating their real cost. Though the government agency responsible for distributing these goods and services received explicit subsidies from the treasury (as did other state agencies), this practice constituted a far more important *implicit* subsidy for consumer goods that did not appear in the budget.

[37] Since the late 1980s, this was partly ameliorated by the "sale" of some oil dollars to importers at higher exchange rates.

[38] *MidEast Markets,* March 4, 1991, p. 3; *MEED,* November 8, 1992, p. 16.

realize that they are not making a profit."[39] Increasing explicit government subsidies in an effort to counteract these price increases and production losses would in turn result in larger budget deficits, with all their adverse consequences.

At the beginning of fiscal 1993, the official exchange rates were formally unified at the floating rate. But there were many exceptions, including the use of the old rates for certain essential imports. The free market rate—to which the floating rate was tied—depreciated rapidly from about 500 rials to the dollar before the devaluation to about 1,500 shortly afterward. With oil revenues being recorded in the budget at a more realistic exchange rate, oil's share of total revenues suddenly "increased" from 11 percent in 1992 to 49 percent in 1993—and by a factor of nine in absolute terms—even though when measured in dollars, 1993 oil export revenues were actually 15 percent *lower* than 1992.[40] In December 1993, the government discontinued the unified exchange rates and their connection to the free market rate. In May 1994, it introduced a new official rate for non-oil exports. The free market rate for the rial fell precipitously (to as much as 6,200 rials to the dollar), partly in reaction to the announcement of U.S. sanctions.

A year later, Tehran issued new regulations for what amounted to two official rates of 1,750 rials and 3,000 rials to the dollar, banned the free market exchange rate fluctuating between 3,400 and 4,500 rials to the dollar (in London and Dubai the rial is even weaker), and required non-oil exporters to exchange foreign currency earnings at an official export rate far below the free market rate.[41] The lower (i.e., more overvalued) rate is for importing essential goods, and other transactions involving the government and those it favors; the higher rate is for non-oil exports (largely from the private sector) and various other imports.[42] Non-oil exporters seek to maximize their earnings by smuggling carpets and pistachios into Dubai, where they can get many more rials per dollar of exports than offered by official Iranian rates. "Just a year ago," a 1995 report stated, "Rafsanjani was talking about abolishing multiple exchange rates, privatizing the economy, and eliminating all subsidies. All this has been abandoned in recent months."[43] In October 1995, the Central Bank vice governor asserted that the president's economic reforms had been postponed, not abandoned. He cautioned that unifying the exchange rates was "a big job" that would take time.[44]

---

[39] *MEED*, December 18, 1992, p. 31.

[40] See Tables 5 and 7. If this were done for *all* foreign exchange receipts, the contribution of oil to the budget (and thus to the economy) would be shown to be much higher.

[41] *Middle East* (December 1994), pp. 28-29; EIU, *Country Report–Iran*, no. 2 (1995), p. 13. Before the change, non-oil exporters were allowed to keep a fraction in dollars.

[42] "Hard Days Ahead for the Iranian Economy," *MEES*, October 2, 1995, p. B1.

[43] DRI/McGraw-Hill, *World Markets Report–Iran* (May 1995).

[44] *MEED*, November 3, 1995, p. 12.

THE CURRENT ACCOUNT BALANCE AND EXTERNAL DEBT

During the 1970s oil boom, commodity imports rose sharply from $1.7 billion in 1970 to $16.7 billion in 1977.[45] Rising incomes during this period stimulated demand for imports of consumer goods, while expanding investment and production necessitated increased imports of capital and intermediate goods. In addition, the shah's military build-up increased arms imports from a mere $160 million in 1970 to $2.6 billion in 1977.[46] Average annual agricultural imports also rose sharply, from $284 million in 1970-73 to $1.6 billion in 1974-78, due in part to a steep increase in world food prices beginning in 1973. Despite a positive current account balance during 1970-77[47] which increased foreign exchange reserves from a mere $76 million in 1970 to nearly $1 billion in 1973 and close to $11 billion by the end of 1977,[48] foreign debt increased rapidly from $6.8 billion in 1973 to $10.7 billion in 1978.

Though the Islamic regime was ideologically opposed to foreign debt and sharply curtailed imports (particularly of luxury goods and arms) until the war, by 1980-81 there was a negative current account balance.[49] Strong oil export revenues in 1982-83 briefly restored the positive current account balance, but it was followed by ten consecutive annual deficits. Despite sharp increases in arms imports during the last five years of the war (1984-88), however, Iran actually reduced its obligations (largely short-term trade credits with a one- or two-year maturity) to $4.3 billion in 1988.

Though oil export revenues increased dramatically after the 1988 ceasefire, imports rose far more rapidly—from $10.6 billion that year to an unprecedented $25.2 billion (and a $10.2 billion current account deficit) in 1991, resulting in a mammoth cumulative deficit of $33.2 billion. This was followed by sizable (albeit smaller) annual deficits of $7.3 billion in 1992 and $4.5 billion in 1993. In 1989, Rafsanjani persuaded the parliament to authorize $17 billion in foreign loans and $10 billion in investment by foreign companies (primarily through joint ventures) to accelerate development.[50] According to the World Bank, Iran's foreign debt rose from $5.8 billion in 1988 to $12.9 billion in 1992, when for the first time it was unable to meet its payment obligations.

---

[45] If imported services, insurance, freight, international travel, interest, and dividend payments to foreigners are included, total imports of goods and services actually increased from $3.1 billion to $25.6 billion.

[46] See Tables 2, 5, and 11; IMF, pp. 170-71, 426-27.

[47] The current account balance is defined as exports of goods and services minus imports, plus (or minus) unilateral transfers. In the case of Iran, most transfers are funds from Iranians abroad to their relatives in Iran. In the early 1990s, the Statistical Bureau estimated that transfers added $2.5 billion annually to the positive side of Iran's balance of payments.

[48] IMF, pp. 424, 427.

[49] Foreign exchange reserves, which peaked at $14.6 billion in 1979, declined to $5.3 billion in 1982; see Table 5.

[50] NYT, May 29, 1991, p. A10.

With a reputation for punctual payments, Tehran had little difficulty convincing lenders to extend more credit. The government embarked on a series of rescheduling negotiations and reached agreements with all its major creditors—Germany, Japan, Italy, France, Austria, Switzerland, and Britain.[51] By fiscal 1994-95, it had restructured 70 percent of its $22.7 billion debt into medium-term (five or six year) loans, which substantially reduced the immediate debt service burden. In 1994, the authorities cut annual commodity imports back drastically from $25.2 billion in 1991 to $12-13 billion in 1994 and 1995, in order to provide the balance of payments surplus required to meet the new schedule of payments.[52] The current account balance reversed sharply from annual deficits averaging $6.7 billion during 1991-93 to surpluses of about $4 billion during 1994-95.[53]

Despite these drastic measures, however, Iran's foreign debt remains beyond the capabilities of its economy to repay. During 1994-95, oil export revenues rose by only $1 billion. Though higher oil prices in 1996 resulted in oil export revenues $2-3 billion above original projections, Iran's foreign debt in late 1996 remained over $20 billion—greater than its annual oil export revenues in recent years.[54] Moreover, Iran is paying a heavy price for its austerity. The constriction of imports has adverse effects on the economy in general and industry in particular, and is an important factor in reducing its rate of growth. Servicing the debt in coming years will require sizable current account surpluses, and in the absence of much higher export earnings or other unforeseen developments, the clerical regime's current policies (which it will probably continue) could translate into severe political upheaval in the future.[55]

---

[51] EIU, *Country Profile–Iran* (1995-96), pp. 46-47.

[52] See Tables 5 and 12.

[53] EIU, *Country Report–Iran*, no. 4 (1996), pp. 5, 26.

[54] *MEES*, January 6, 1997, p. 85.

[55] See *MEED*, August 18, 1995, p. 5.

IX

Conclusions

On the eve of the thirteenth anniversary of the revolution in February 1992, President Rafsanjani promised his people that within two or three years a "new Iran" would emerge that would be both prosperous and powerful.[1] Instead, the large majority of Iranians continued to suffer from low wages, rapid inflation, stagnant or declining living standards, and a widening gap between themselves and a small, wealthy elite. In ceremonies three years later celebrating the sixteenth anniversary of the revolution, the president tried to explain the economic failures by blaming the West and particularly the United States,[2] and warned the public not to be taken in by the West's "poisonous campaign of lies."[3] In reality, most of Iran's economic problems are of its own making, such as unrealistic exchange rates, excessive subsidies, rampant corruption, politically motivated mismanagement, and other obstacles to reform and development.

ECONOMIC DISTORTIONS

Multiple Exchange Rates. A 1992 study concluded that the yawning gap between the free market exchange rate and the system of multiple official exchange rates adopted and expanded in the 1980s accounts for many if not most of the severe economic distortions afflicting the Iranian economy. The study observed that such a gap results in

> the overinvoicing of imports and underinvoicing of exports, [which] deprives the government of foreign exchange revenues, encourages capital transfers abroad, and generally erodes public confidence in the government's management of the economy.... [In addition, it] promotes corruption and results in considerable misallocation of resources primarily from manufacturing to trade and distribution and a significant bias against investment [in industry].[4]

---

[1] *Middle East Economic Digest* (*MEED*), February 21, 1992, p. iii.

[2] *Financial Times* (*FT*), May 2, 1995, p. 4.

[3] Since the April 1995 U.S. ban on trade with Iran, Iran's political and religious leaders cast the blame for its worsening economic problems on the "Great Satan," the United States. Ayatollah Khameini, for example, said "The [U.S.] enemy wishes [Iran] to have inflation. The enemy wishes this country's money to be worthless"; see *New York Times* (*NYT*), February 12, 1995, p. 14.

[4] M. Hashem Pesaran, "The Iranian Foreign Exchange Policy and the Black Market for Dollars," *International Journal for Middle Eastern Studies* 24, no. 1 (February 1992), pp. 101-21.

It also noted the powerful impediments to change:

> A rationalization of the exchange rate system [i.e., to a uniform, market-oriented exchange rate] . . . inevitably involves short-run costs in the form of higher inflation and political alienation of groups who are the main beneficiaries of the current system—namely, the importers, the merchants, and their allies and associates in the government and the clerical hierarchy.[5]

In addition to powerful interest groups that have amassed great fortunes through access (determined largely by personal "connections" and bribery) to overvalued exchange rates, the majority of the population lives near or below the poverty line and has come to depend on food and other necessities that are implicitly "subsidized" by being imported at the most favorable exchange rate. The 1995-96 foreign exchange budget for non-oil exports was $4.9 billion, compared to $4.5 billion the previous year. The change in policy from liberalization and incentives to harsh controls and punishments meted out to those dealing in the black market has clouded the outlook for increasing non-oil exports.[6] The system of exchange controls induces Iranians to keep their funds beyond the reach and control of Iranian authorities.[7] Though there are no authoritative estimates, unofficial reports indicate that the bulk of private non-oil export earnings is kept abroad. One 1995 estimate suggested that these holdings may be as high as $180 billion.[8] If even 10 percent of these funds were repatriated and invested in Iran, its economy would boom.

Instead of offering incentives to private sector investment, however, the government appears to be moving away from liberalization toward more repressive controls. It expanded the list of price-controlled goods to encompass hundreds of products including cars and appliances, and announced new exchange rates accompanied by a regulation requiring non-oil exporters to sell all hard currency earnings at the Central Bank rate. Mobile courts were established to punish merchants and currency dealers who violated the new decrees, and the free market for currency was driven into the black market.[9] In addition, intense social pressure was exerted on price control violators. In a January 1995 Friday sermon, Ayatollah Jannati declared that "blood-sucking capitalists should be whipped."[10] Not to be outdone, Rafsanjani blamed inflation on shopkeepers and called them "bloodsucking leeches."[11]

---

[5] Ibid.

[6] "Hard Days Ahead for the Iranian Economy," *Middle East Economic Survey* (*MEES*), October 2, 1995, p. B1.

[7] *MEED*, February 17, 1995, p. 22.

[8] Ibid., January 13, 1994, p. 9. By comparison, 1994 oil exports were less than $15 billion.

[9] *MEED MONEY*, May 26, 1995, p. 6.

[10] *MEED*, February 10, 1995, p. 21.

[11] *Wall Street Journal* (*WSJ*), May 11, 1995, pp. A1, A13.

Implicit and Explicit Subsidies. In 1994, President Rafsanjani stated that the annual cost of government subsidies (both implicit and explicit) was about $15 billion, roughly equal to Iran's oil export revenues that year.[12] According to Rafsanjani, without subsidies the price of bread would be twenty times higher.[13] Like exchange rates, these various subsidies distort the economy, constitute a very heavy burden on the national treasury, and increase deficit spending and its attendant effects on inflation and the balance of payments. The excessive growth in consumption stimulated by below-market domestic prices reduces the surplus available for export and thereby foreign exchange earnings. And, like the multiple exchange rates policy, the government's frequent efforts to reduce these subsidies have been thwarted by powerful opposition.[14]

External Debt. Iran's foreign debt has grown rapidly since 1989. During the long and costly war with Iraq, the government resisted recourse to foreign loans for ideological reasons and actually *reduced* its external debt. Rafsanjani effectively abandoned this policy, however, and Iran's foreign debt has more than quadrupled since 1988. The problem was not only the size but the nature of the debt: 90 percent was short-term (1-2 year) credit, and the burden of repaying both principal and interest proved too heavy. By 1992, Iran was facing the prospect of defaulting and its major creditors had little choice but to reschedule the repayment period to 5-6 years in order to reduce the size of current payments. The change is not without consequences, however; in order to finance both needed imports and debt obligations, export earnings will have to rise strongly and/or Iran will have to harshly restrict imports (which almost inevitably has a recessionary effect on the economy) at least until the end of the decade.

With little change in both oil and non-oil exports in recent years, Iran had already begun to restrict imports in 1995.[15] If it implemented reforms in exchange rate controls and subsidies as it has been urged to do by the IMF and some of its own economists, import demand would naturally be constrained and non-oil exports would rise more rapidly. But these reforms appear to be stymied by internal political conflict, powerful interest groups, and other influential people who benefit enormously from the status quo.

Privatization. IMF experts and others have similarly urged the Iranian authorities to privatize state-owned enterprises in order to improve productivity and efficiency, reduce the need for massive government subsidies, and raise incomes. Though Iran's inefficient and frequently

---

[12] Economist Intelligence Unit (EIU), *Country Report–Iran,* no. 2 (1994), p. 17; see also *MEED,* June 3, 1994, p. 29.

[13] *NYT,* April 14, 1992, p. A5. Despite such heavy subsidies, 43 percent of Iranian children under five years old suffer from malnutrition; see EIU, *Country Profile–Iran* (1994-95), p. 15.

[14] In those instances when it has persuaded the parliament to lower the oil subsidy (i.e., increase prices), rising inflation subsequently reduces the real domestic price again; see *Gulf States Newsletter,* June 19, 1995, p. 8.

[15] Reuters, December 18, 1995.

corrupt bureaucracy stymied efforts to restructure or privatize large state enterprises operating at a loss,[16] the government began privatizing small enterprises in 1991. The Industrial Development and Renovation Organization, the state agency which oversaw privatization, reportedly sold some fifty factories for $140 million through the Tehran stock exchange between 1991 and 1994. It suspended further privatization measures, however, because of demands by the parliament that those who had made sacrifices for the revolution be rewarded with shares at half the market price.[17] In addition, the government became "alarmed" at the prospect of further unemployment, which is the inevitable short-term consequence of privatization as redundant workers are fired by private owners who do not receive the subsidies given to state-owned enterprises. In fact, various laws hamper efforts to fire redundant workers, which makes the private sector reluctant to purchase state-owned enterprises with their bloated staffs.

OBSTACLES TO REFORM

The Bonyads. A major obstacle to privatization unique to Iran is the powerful *bonyads.* The Islamic government established these "charitable" foundations under the control of the Muslim clergy to provide for the needy and gave them the industrial enterprises and other property that belonged to the shah and his supporters. The heads of the *bonyads* are understandably reluctant to give up any of their enterprises to privatization, and the government has little control over them.[18]

Manpower Policies. The system of labor and management that has evolved since the revolution is another major obstacle to economic reform. Iran suffered a severe blow when hundreds of thousands of skilled managers and other professionals fled the revolution. Efficiency and productivity were further undermined by post-revolution policies that reserve senior government positions, management of state enterprises, and nearly half of all university openings for those deemed politically (and therefore Islamically) "correct."[19] As a result, unqualified candidates are appointed to manage enterprises despite "widespread weakness in basic management skills."[20] Similarly, certain students are exempt from taking the standard entrance exams.[21] These policies lower professional and academic standards and promote mediocrity rather than excellence.

---

[16] *MEED*, February 11, 1994, p. 8.

[17] Ibid., February 10, 1995, pp. 8-15.

[18] *Sunday Telegraph*, August 16, 1995.

[19] *WSJ*, May 11, 1995, pp. A1, A13. The government bureaucracy has grown inordinately since the revolution, mostly as a means of reducing unemployment. This contributes to budget deficits, which translate into inflation and balance of payments problems.

[20] *Financial Times/Survey–Iran*, February 8, 1993, p. i.

[21] Jahangir Amuzegar, *Iran's Economy under the Islamic Republic* (London: I.B. Taurus & Co., 1993), p. 68.

Corruption. In an interview shortly before his death in 1994, Mehdi Bazargan, Iran's first post-revolution prime minister, described the scale of corruption as "breathtaking." Though corruption is hardly unique to Iran, price controls and the wide gap between the various official rates provide tempting opportunities for corrupt practices.[22] In 1995, the *Financial Times* reported that "exporters with access to foreign currency have become very rich [while the] masses who earn rials find that their income and living standards have dropped drastically."[23] According to another report,

> the inability of Iranians to make ends meet has contributed to rampant corruption. During the monarchy, aides to the shah got rich on government contracts. Today corruption extends to every level of the government, from the heads of foundations [*bonyads*] which import goods and hand out contracts, to the traffic police and garbage collectors. In the shah's time it was only the top echelon. Now everyone has to be paid.[24]

In some respects, the government appears to encourage practices that would be considered immoral or at least improper in other societies. Young men, for example, are legally permitted to buy their way out of compulsory military service. Similarly, the government sells permits to motorists that allow them to violate Tehran's traffic rules. In a sense, corruption has been institutionalized—"Every transaction with the government has now acquired . . . [a] price."[25]

The result, observed one report, "is a steady degradation of the ideals that brought the revolutionary leaders to power, an inefficiency that has strangled the economy, and a cynicism that has fueled corruption."[26] This phenomenon is not limited to the secular bureaucracy; according to another report, many members of "the Islamic hierarchy have succumbed to the lures of high living and corruption . . . while the bulk of the population is being impoverished due to rising inflation and unemployment."[27] Nor is this a new problem. Ayatollah Khomeini warned clerics to give up their "luxurious foreign lifestyles and fancy cars,"[28] but was apparently ignored.

OIL TO THE RESCUE?

Oil has been the overwhelming determinant of Iran's economic health since at least the 1970s. Notwithstanding plans for diversification, Iran's

---

[22] See Chapter VII.

[23] *FT*, May 24, 1995, p. 6.

[24] *NYT*, May 20, 1995, pp. A1, A8.

[25] Amuzegar, p. 318.

[26] *NYT*, May 20, 1995, pp. A1, A8.

[27] *Middle East* (July 1993), pp. 13-15.

[28] *Middle East Review* (1992), p. 50.

cycle of economic expansion and recession continues to depend almost entirely on oil production, world oil prices, and oil export revenues.[29] Yet despite efforts to expand oil production, Iranian output has been static at 3.7 MBD since 1993.[30] With the volume of oil exports unchanged and prices down from their post-Gulf War peak, the trend in the Iranian economy since 1993 has been recessionary—flat or negative *per capita* GDP growth.[31] Oil industry sources dismiss Iranian claims that it is deliberately producing under its sustainable capacity of 4.1 MBD in accordance with OPEC quotas, noting that Iran's current output is close to its sustainable capacity of about 3.8 MBD.[32] Considering Iran's past performance and current financial problems, it would not hesitate to ignore its OPEC quota (as other members of the organization do) if it could.[33]

The constraints on Iran's oil production appear to be financial and technological rather than political—it lacks the necessary technical expertise and foreign exchange to invest in expanding capacity. The mass flight of adequately trained managerial and technical personnel (both domestic and foreign) following the revolution, and the effects of the war with Iraq, continue to impede the performance of the oil industry and other economic sectors. The obvious solution, from a purely economic point of view, is the participation of Western oil companies which possess both capital and advanced technology. In this regard, however, the impediments *are* political: as was true of other developing countries during the 1960s and 1970s, Iran nationalized foreign oil companies and canceled their concessions. Though Tehran has sought foreign investment in its less politically sensitive *offshore* oil, this accounts for only about 10 percent of total oil revenues, and in the current political climate in Iran, advocacy of onshore investment remains tantamount to political suicide.

At the same time, the long-term trend in oil prices (measured in inflation-adjusted dollars) has been and will continue to be downward.[34] The eventual end of UN sanctions on Iraqi oil exports, and increasing exports from the former Soviet Union (which was the world's largest oil

---

[29] Iran's huge reserves of natural gas (second only to those of Russia) are not easily marketed due to logistical reasons—namely, the geographic distance from Iran to big gas markets in Western Europe, the Far East, and the United States. Iran's policy is to increase domestic use of natural gas in order to free more oil for export. The idea of constructing gas pipelines to Europe and/or the Indian subcontinent has been discussed from time to time, but the political and economic impediments are formidable. There is little prospect of significant growth in gas exports in the foreseeable future, and thus Iran's dependence on oil exports will continue to be overwhelming.

[30] *Petroleum Economist*, December 1996, p. 63.

[31] See Table 12.

[32] *MEED*, June 2, 1995, p. 7; see also *Petroleum Intelligence Weekly*, May 29, 1995, p. 6.

[33] *Middle East* (January 1993), p. 19; (June 1993), pp. 27-29.

[34] See Eliyahu Kanovsky, *OPEC Ascendant? Another Case of Crying Wolf*, Policy Paper no. 20 (Washington, DC: Washington Institute for Near East Policy, 1990), and *The Economic Consequences of the Persian Gulf War: Accelerating OPEC's Demise*, Policy Paper no. 30 (Washington, DC: Washington Institute for Near East Policy, 1992), especially pp. 71-103.

producer and a major exporter until neglect and political turmoil led to a sharp drop in production), will further depress prices.[35]

Though exogenous events such as revolutions, wars, or other disturbances in one or more of the oil-exporting countries in the Middle East or elsewhere may temporarily boost oil prices, they will inevitably fall back to or below "pre-event" levels, as demonstrated by the Persian Gulf War. Thus, unless Iran radically changes its policies on foreign participation in developing its oil resources and massively subsidizing domestic oil consumption, it faces a period of stagnant or even declining oil exports—at a time when the revenues from these exports will continue to be the basis of its economy.

THE EFFICACY OF U.S. SANCTIONS

The U.S. government has branded Iran an "outlaw state" bent on terrorism and nuclear blackmail. In April 1995, President Clinton announced a total trade embargo against Iran. He has also pressured (with only marginal success) Russian president Boris Yeltsin to cancel plans to sell nuclear technology to Iran, which Tehran and Moscow claim is for generating electricity and desalination only.[36] In view of its largely underutilized gas reserves, there is little economic rationale for Iran to build a nuclear reactor. Hence the suspicion that its goals are political and military rather than economic.

Some observers have argued that the U.S. embargo has had little impact on Iran's economy because other major industrialized countries are not only not participating in it, but are happily making the business deals that American firms are compelled to refuse, such as the Conoco offshore oil deal. In fact, recent reports indicate that Washington's so-called "dual containment" policy is having tangible effects.[37] Japan, for example, has reportedly suspended indefinitely the second installment of funding for the huge Karun dam project—and ruled out further credits at favorable interest rates—out of concern that this could lead to political friction with Washington.[38] In addition to hindering investment in Iran, U.S. pressure has led reportedly to the suspension of some activites of concern to Washington, such as nuclear cooperation.[39]

---

[35] Exports from the former Soviet Union fell from 12.6 MBD in 1987 to 7.1 MBD in 1994, when they began to rise again. Production in the first half of 1995 was 3 percent higher than during the same period in 1994; see *Petroleum Economist* (October 1995), p. 5. According to Western oil executives, oil exploration and extraction in the former Soviet Union has not even begun to realize its potential.

[36] *WSJ*, May 11, 1995, pp. A1, A13.

[37] See footnote 20 in chapter II.

[38] EIU, *Country Report–Iran*, no. 1 (1991), p. 28.

[39] Ibid., p. 25.

Critics of U.S. policy also fail to take into account its indirect effects. The mere announcement of the trade ban triggered a sharp devaluation of the rial on the free market.[40] Moreover, the United States had been an important market for Iranian oil, and Tehran reportedly had difficulty redistributing the roughly 500,000 barrels of oil it sold to the United States every day, which in turn had a marginal effect on the price it obtained for its oil.[41] Similarly, the United States remains the world's primary—and in some cases *sole*—source of oil field equipment and spare parts.[42] Of the $340 million in U.S. exports to Iran in 1994 (i.e., before the embargo), 50 percent were from oil service contractors.[43]

Overall, the cancellation of the Conoco deal signalled potential investors—American and others—that Iran's economy had not emerged from the political shadow of its governement, and in itself contributed to the general feeling of pessimism in Tehran.[44] In short, U.S. sanctions are an additional blow to an economy that is already reeling from the aftermath of the revolution, the Iran-Iraq War, and above all its leaders' inability to adopt and enforce policies that could eventually lead to economic development and even prosperity.

MILITARY SPENDING

When the leaders of the Islamic revolution took power in 1979, they cut back sharply on the shah's large-scale orders of military equipment from the United States and other countries, and then quickly reversed that policy when the war with Iraq started. Following the 1988 ceasefire, Iran began to rebuild its armed forces, purchasing arms from Russia, China, Brazil, Argentina, Pakistan, and others.[45] There is evidence, however, of cuts in military spending since 1992 or 1993 that probably reflect the country's economic difficulties. According to one researcher, Iran allocated about $2 billion annually for arms imports during 1988-91. This was reduced to about $1 billion in 1992 and then further in 1993. Another researcher noted that Iran canceled more than $5 billion in arms deals in 1993.[46] According to a U.S. Congressional Research Service report, Iranian

---

[40] Ibid., no. 2 (1995), p. 7.

[41] *MEED*, August 25, 1995, p. 20.

[42] *FT*, May 16, 1995, p. 8.

[43] EIU, *Country Report–Iran*, no. 2 (1995), p. 9.

[44] *NYT*, May 16, 1995, p. A6. Oil Minister Gholam Reza Aqazedeh was reportedly "devastated" by the cancellation; see *WSJ*, May 11, 1995, p. A13.

[45] There are also reports of deliveries of missiles from North Korea; see Joseph S. Bermudez, Jr., *Proliferation for Profit: North Korea in the Middle East*, Policy Focus no. 27 (Washington, DC: Washington Institute for Near East Policy, 1994); *FT*, February 6, 1992, p. 4; *MEED*, February 21, 1992, p. 12; *NYT*, March 6, 1992, p. A10.

[46] Patrick Clawson, *Iran's Strategic Intentions and Capabilities* (Washington, DC: National Defense University, 1994), pp. 73, 100.

arms imports amounted to a total of $8.6 billion during 1986-89, fell to $5.3 billion during 1990-93,[47] then to $850 million in 1993-94,[48] and have been the same or slightly higher in recent years.[49]

None of this suggests that economic difficulties have or will put an end to Iran's role as an "international sponsor of terrorism," as U.S. Secretary of State Warren Christopher has described Iran.[50] Indeed, considerable evidence suggests that Iran continues to invest significant resources in support for terrorism and the pursuit of weapons of mass destruction.[51] Cuts in conventional military spending since 1992 indicate that there is some (albeit limited) relationship between the state of the economy and decisions regarding military expenditures. Moreover, Iranian leaders may have learned from the collapse of the Soviet Union that, without economic strength, military strength is a mirage.

POLITICAL REPERCUSSIONS

Periodic violent outbursts by Iranian citizens who are frustrated by and angry at the nation's deepening economic problems may make the regime think twice before it expends resources for presumable political or military gain. A 1990 report noted that "[r]ioting in Tehran and provincial cities has emerged against the daily grind of volatile prices, poverty, and squalid housing conditions."[52] In 1991, riots erupted again in several of Iran's big cities. The *Economist* reported that Rafsanjani tried to quell the disturbances by reminding the "malcontents that the purges of the early years of the revolution could yet return." But Rafsanjani's

> main vulnerability has been his own wealth. He is believed to have huge business interests and to operate a system of patronage that excludes the unfavored from big dealerships and contracts. His sons are said to control more than 400 companies. [But] the economy's poor performance is catching up with him, and the excuse of the eight-year war [with Iraq] is wearing thin.[53]

---

[47] The figures are in current dollars (i.e., not adjusted for dollar inflation); see Richard F. Grimmett, *Conventional Arms Transfers to the Third World: 1986-93*, CRS Report No. 94-612F (Washington, DC: Congressional Research Service, 1994).

[48] See *Iran Brief*, December 4, 1995, p. 11.

[49] International Monetary Fund, *Islamic Republic of Iran–Statistical Appendix* (October 1996), p. 24.

[50] *NYT*, May 1, 1995, p. 1; see also Christopher's remarks in *Fighting Terrorism, Waging Peace: Twin Challenges for Democracies and Peacemakers* (proceedings of a conference sponsored by the Washington Institute for Near East Policy, May 20-21, 1996).

[51] See Michael Eisenstadt, *Iranian Military Power: Capabilities and Intentions*, Policy Paper no. 42 (Washington, DC: Washington Institute for Near East Policy, 1996).

[52] *FT*, March 6, 1990, p. 4.

[53] *Economist*, July 11, 1992, p. 45.

Riots in 1992 were much more violent. In the city of Mashad, 100 government buildings, banks, shops, and cars were burned or wrecked. "Criticism of the government [was] being voiced throughout the country . . . . The economic depression was having a cumulative effect on the poverty-stricken majority . . . [who] are economically considerably worse off now than [under] the shah."[54] This time the regime reacted with harsh measures. Some rioters in Shiraz and Mashad were tried in an Islamic court and sentenced to prison terms, flogging, or execution.[55] Despite harsh punishment, sporadic rioting continues to erupt. A 1995 report said that "[d]ozens of Iranians have been killed in spontaneous riots in recent years, mostly by special forces that have been called in when local police would not open fire . . . . [L]ong lines for subsidized food breed despair." After doubling fuel prices in March of that year, the government posted armed guards at gas stations and strengthened its internal security forces.[56]

A 1996 IMF mission to Iran concluded that the economy "remains fragile, too dependent on oil, and in need of reforms,"[57] which have "proceeded in fits and starts, with the government passing one piece of legislation . . . and then passing further legislation undermining the first."[58] Whereas Ayatollah Khomeini's authority was unchallenged, unpopular decisions have proved difficult to make since his death.[59] Rafsanjani's economic reform proposals such as private enterprise, cuts in subsidies, and other painful measures have often been challenged by Ayatollah Ali Khamene'i, Iran's more ideological supreme leader, who favors popular "social justice"—more subsidies and public services, drastic cuts in imports of luxury goods, harsh measures against civil servants who take bribes, and measures to "prevent the amassing of fortunes overnight."[60] Thus, while the deterioration of the economy has eroded public support for the government in general,[61] the religious leaders have increasingly blamed the nation's ills on Rafsanjani and the "Western-oriented technocrats" who favor his reform proposals.[62] As a result, support for Rafsanjani seems to be declining as Khamene'i gains in popularity.[63]

[54] *Gulf States Newsletter,* June 15, 1992, pp. 2-3; June 29, 1992, p. 5.

[55] *MEED,* June 26, 1992, p. 23.

[56] *WSJ,* May 11, 1995, pp. A1, A13. For more on Iranian domestic politics, see David Menashri, *Revolution at a Crossroads: Iran's Domestic Politics and Regional Ambitions,* Policy Paper no. 43 (Washington, DC: Washington Institute for Near East Policy, 1997).

[57] *MEES,* December 23/30, 1996, p. B5.

[58] EIU, *Country Profile–Iran* (1996-97), pp. 11-14.

[59] *Economist,* February 12, 1994, p. 42.

[60] *Middle East* (February 1995), p. 12; *EIU Country Report–Iran,* no. 1 (1994), p. 17.

[61] In a 1994 interview, Mehdi Bazargan, the first post-revolution prime minister, stated that the government enjoyed the support of less than 5 percent of the people; see *NYT,* May 20, 1995, pp. A1, A8.

[62] *WSJ,* June 28, 1994, pp. A1, A12.

[63] In the 1989 presidential elections, Rafsanjani received about 90 percent of the vote; in 1993, his support declined to about 60 percent; see *Middle East* (January 1994), p. 10.

Higher oil prices in 1996 benefited Iran but did not improve the ability of the leadership to implement basic reforms or alter underlying economic trends. According to a January 1997 assessment, "[e]conomic mismanagement [and] pervasive corruption [continue to] hold back economic growth and investment" in Iran, while inflation-adjusted "incomes have sunk savagely, particularly for the disappearing middle class."[64] As a result, the annual rate of economic growth since 1993 has averaged 1.5 percent, well below the 3 percent annual growth in population. In other words, *per capita* GDP has been declining since 1993, and projections for 1997 and 1998 indicate a continuation of the trend. This implies deteriorating employment capacity and a further drop in living standards for the large majority of Iranians. If, as anticipated, oil prices decline from the unusually high levels in 1996, Iran's economic troubles will multiply.

Iran's poor economic performance is due largely to policies that are adverse to sustained economic growth, and the short-term outlook is for further deterioration. The Rafsanjani government may muddle through until the 1997 presidential elections, "relying on coercion to ensure domestic order."[65] But despite strengthening internal security forces, the deteriorating economy and mounting unrest suggest the possibility that at some point, the bubble will burst and Iran's clerical leadership will face more radical and possibly more violent economic and political change. Some have speculated that the army may take over; others say that the opposition in exile may seize power.[66] In any event, these changes will have important political, military, and strategic ramifications for the Persian Gulf region and for the Middle East as a whole.

According to unofficial sources, Rafsanjani survived a seventh assassination attempt in February 1994; see *Economist,* June 25, 1994, pp. 45-46.

[64] *Economist/ Survey–Iran,* January 18, 1997, pp. 1-16.

[65] Shahram Chubin, *Iran's National Security Policy* (Washington, DC: Carnegie Endowment for International Peace, 1994), p. 78.

[66] *Economist,* February 12, 1994, p. 42.

Appendices

Table 1

OIL PRODUCTION

(in millions of barrels per day)

1973–83

	1973	1974	1975	1976	1977	1978	1979	1980	1981	1982	1983
Saudi Arabia	7.7	8.6	7.2	8.8	9.4	8.6	9.8	10.3	10.2	6.9	5.4
Kuwait	3.1	2.6	2.1	2.2	2	2.2	2.6	1.7	1.2	0.9	1.1
United Arab Emirates	1.5	1.7	1.7	1.9	2	1.8	1.8	1.7	1.5	1.3	1.2
Iraq	2	2	2.3	2.4	2.4	2.6	3.5	2.6	0.9	1	1.1
Qatar	0.6	0.5	0.4	0.5	0.4	0.5	0.5	0.5	0.4	0.3	0.3
Libya	2.2	1.5	1.5	1.9	2.1	2	2.1	1.8	1.2	1.2	1.1
Algeria	1.1	1	1	1.1	1.1	1.2	1.2	1.2	1.1	1	1
OAPEC (Arab members of OPEC)	18.2	17.9	16.2	18.8	19.5	18.8	21.6	19.7	16.4	12.5	11.1
Iran	5.9	6.1	5.4	5.9	5.7	5.3	3.2	1.5	1.3	2.4	2.5
Middle East OPEC (OAPEC plus Iran)	24.1	24	21.6	24.7	25.2	24.1	24.7	21.2	17.7	14.9	13.6
OPEC	31.3	31.1	27.5	31.1	31.7	30.3	31.5	27.5	23.4	20	18.4
World Production	58.5	58.6	55.7	60.1	62.6	63.1	65.8	62.8	59.4	57.1	56.7
USA	11	10.5	10	9.7	9.9	10.3	10.1	10.2	10.2	10.2	10.5
Former Soviet Union (FSU)	8.7	9.3	9.9	10.5	11.1	11.6	11.9	12.2	12.4	12.4	12.5
Non-OPEC production (excludes USA and FSU)	7.6	7.8	8.2	8.7	10	10.9	12.3	13	13.5	14.6	15.6

1984–94

	1984	1985	1986	1987	1988	1989	1990	1991	1992	1993	1994
Saudi Arabia	4.6	3.7	5.3	4.7	5.9	5.8	7.3	9	9.3	9.1	9
Kuwait	1.2	1.1	1.4	1.1	1.5	1.6	1.3	0.2	1.1	1.9	2.1
United Arab Emirates	1.3	1.3	1.6	1.6	1.6	2	2.3	2.6	2.5	2.5	2.5
Iraq	1.2	1.4	1.9	2.4	2.8	2.8	2.2	0.3	0.5	0.5	0.5
Qatar	0.4	0.3	0.4	0.3	0.4	0.4	0.4	0.4	0.5	0.5	0.5
Libya	1	1.1	1.1	1	1.1	1.2	1.4	1.5	1.5	1.4	1.4
Algeria	1	1.1	1.2	1.2	1.3	1.3	1.3	1.3	1.3	1.3	1.3
OAPEC (Arab members of OPEC)	10.8	10.5	12.7	12.3	14.4	15.1	16.2	15.4	16.7	17.1	17.2
Iran	2.1	2.2	2.1	2.3	2.3	2.9	3.3	3.5	3.5	3.6	3.6
Middle East OPEC (OAPEC plus Iran)	12.9	12.7	14.8	14.6	16.7	17.9	19.5	18.9	20.2	20.7	20.8
OPEC	17.8	17	20	19.5	21.7	23.3	25.3	25.3	26.5	27.1	27.3
World Production	57.7	57.6	60.7	60.9	63.5	64.4	66	65.6	66	66	66.7
USA	10.5	10.6	10.2	9.9	9.8	9.2	8.9	9.1	8.9	8.6	8.4
Former Soviet Union (FSU)	12.3	12	12.4	12.7	12.6	12.4	11.6	10.5	9.1	8.2	7.4
Non-OPEC production (excludes USA and FSU)	17.1	18	18.3	18.8	19.4	19.5	20.2	20.8	21.4	22.1	23.7

Sources: British Petroleum, *Statistical Review of World Energy* (London: British Petroleum Co.), June 1995 and earlier issues. Note: The other members of OPEC are Venezuela, Nigeria, Gabon, and Indonesia (Ecuador and Gabon withdrew in the mid-1990s).

Table 2

IRAN'S MILITARY BURDEN[2]

1973–82

	1973	1974	1975	1976	1977	1978	1979	1980	1981	1982
Military expenditures (% of GNP)	8.3	13.8	17.6	15.6	11.9	15.3	7.9	7	6.8	6.4
Arms imports (in millions of U.S. dollars)	525	1,000	1,200	2,000	2,600	2,100	1,500	420	925	1,600
Armed forces (in thousands)	285	310	385	420	350	350	415	305	260	240
Armed forces (per thousand)	9.1	9.6	11.5	12.2	9.9	9.6	11	7.8	6.5	5.7

1983–93

	1983	1984	1985	1986	1987	1988	1989	1990	1991	1992	1993
Military expendit. (% of GNP)	6.1	7.1	7.2	10.3	8.7	8.3	6.4	5.9	5.7	–	–
Arms imports (millions of U.S. $)	825	2700	1,900	2,600	2,000	2,500	1,300	1,400	1,600	2,300	1,000
Armed forces (in thousands)	240	335	345	345	350	654	604	440	465	–	–
Armed forces (per thousand)	5.5	7.5	7.5	7	6.8	12.3	11	7.7	7.9	–	–

Sources: U.S. Arms Control and Disarmament Agency, *World Military Expenditures and Arms Transfers*, 1991–92 and earlier.
Notes: Iran's outlays for arms imports are assumed to be at least partially "off budget." Estimates for the armed forces appear to exclude the Revolutionary Guard and other irregular forces, which played a major role in the war with Iraq (1980–88). The near doubling of the armed forces from 1987 to 1988 (the year of the ceasefire) is of doubtful validity.

Table 3

INFLATION AND IRANIAN LIVING STANDARDS

1973–83

	1973	1974	1975	1976	1977	1978	1979	1980	1981	1982	1983
Annual % change—implicit GDP deflator	34.4	60.9	10.6	13	17.7	10.3	27.1	29.1	23.8	16.4	12.1
—wholesale price index	11.2	16.8	7.8	9.2	17.1	10.1	14.1	31.1	23.6	12.8	14.7
—consumer price index	9.9	14.7	12.8	10.9	27.6	11.7	10.5	20.6	24.2	18.7	19.7
Private consumption (*in billions of 1990 rials*)	12,348	14,937	16,067	18,879	21,405	17,879	19,529	18,882	20,056	21,533	23,548
Population (*in millions*)	31.23	32.5	33.38	33.71	34.69	36.11	37.2	39.3	40.85	42.48	44
Index of real *per capita* private consumption (1990=100)	89.5	104.1	109	126.8	139.8	112.1	118.9	108.8	111.2	114.8	121
% change in real *per capita* private consump.	11.5	16.3	4.7	16.3	10.3	-19.8	6.1	-8.5	2.2	3.2	5.4

1984–94

	1984	1985	1986	1987	1988	1989	1990	1991	1992	1993	1994
Annual % change—implicit GDP deflator	9.7	6.3	21.2	21.5	22.4	20.5	18.6	23.6	24.9	38.4	36.3
—wholesale price index	7.7	5.3	19	32.3	22.2	20.3	23.9	26.6	33.4	25.3	42.4
—consumer price index	12.5	4.4	18.4	28.6	28.7	22.3	9	20.7	24.4	22.9	35.2
Private consumption (*in billions of 1990 rials*)	24,062	24,812	22,743	20,722	19,639	19,858	22,666	27,510	26,716	31,344	27,913
Population (*in millions*)	45.8	47.82	49.44	50.66	51.91	53.19	54.5	55.84	57.15	58.49	59.78
Index of real *per capita* private consumption (1990=100)	119	117.5	104.2	92.5	85.5	84.4	100	118.5	112.4	128.9	112.4
% change in real *per capita* private consump.	-1.7	-1.3	-11.3	-11.2	-7.6	-1.3	18.5	18.5	-5.1	14.7	-12.8

Sources: International Monetary Fund, *International Financial Statistics*, various issues; Central Bank of Iran, *Annual Report*, various issues. Notes: Gross Domestic product (GDP) deflators and estimates for private consumption are based on a fiscal year beginning March 21; wholesale and consumer price indices are based on years beginning December 21. Real private consumption (RPC) usually reflects living standards. RPC in 1990 prices was derived by using the consumer price index to correct estimates of private consumption in current prices in the national accounts; the three-month discrepancy between the years used for estimating the national accounts and the consumer price index is not significant over the long term.

Table 4

IRANIAN ENERGY PRODUCTION AND CONSUMPTION[4]

1973–83

	1973	1974	1975	1976	1977	1978	1979	1980	1981	1982	1983
Crude oil production (*thousands of barrels/day*)	5,942	5,904	5,249	6,019	5,586	4,252	3,433	1,482	1,474	2,684	2,709
Domestic oil consumption (*thousands b/d*)	276	3,18	378	442	509	517	543	526	545	583	720
Natural gas production (*billions of cubic meters*)	48.7	49.3	44.6	52.3	59.5	44.4	41.7	16.6	15.7	30.4	27.8
Domestic natural gas consumption (*billions m³*)	12.1	12.8	12.3	14	23.9	16.6	21.4	9.4	9.7	18	15.5
Natural gas exports (*billions m³*)	8.6	9.2	9.6	9.3	9.2	5.3	3.5	—	—	—	—
Electricity production (*millions of kilowatt/hours*)	12,093	14,005	15,700	17,235	18,955	19,847	21,909	22,380	24,906	29,076	33,629
Electric power consumption (*millions of kw/h*)	7,796	9,152	10,442	11,734	13,066	14,145	15,917	16,381	18,234	21,753	25,153

1984–94

	1984	1985	1986	1987	1988	1989	1990	1991	1992	1993	1994
Crude oil production (*thousands of b/d*)	2,371	2,504	2,176	2,460	2,557	2,947	3,231	3,366	3,692	3,609	3,603
Domestic oil consumption (*thousands of b/d*)	779	848	789	806	839	881	918	980	1,077	1,125	1,159
Natural gas production (*billions of cubic meters*)	30.9	34.4	25.3	30.9	30.7	32.2	37	46.2	48	48.4	54.9
Domestic gas consumption (*billions m³*)	21.5	24.1	15.6	20.3	20.2	21.3	23.5	32.2	35.1	36.9	43.8
Natural gas exports (*billions cubic meters*)	—	—	—	—	—	—	2.1	2.9	0.5	—	0.1
Electricity production (*millions of kilowatt/hours*)	37,338	40,071	42,548	46,197	47,600	52,712	59,102	64,126	68,419	76,014	—
Electricity consumption (*millions of kilowatt/h*)	28,177	30,812	32,619	34,740	36,147	39,956	45,107	49,175	—	—	—

Sources: Central Bank of Iran, *Economic Report and Balance Sheet*, various issues. Notes: A dispute between Iran and the Soviet Union suspended natural gas exports from 1980–90. The difference between natural gas production and domestic consumption (plus exports where relevant) is flared—i.e., burned off during oil extraction.

Table 5

IRANIAN EXTERNAL ACCOUNTS[5]
(in millions of U.S. dollars)

1973–83

	1973	1974	1975	1976	1977	1978	1979	1980	1981	1982	1983
Merchandise exports	6,122	21,356	20,432	24,719	24,076	17,675	24,171	12,338	11,831	20,452	21,507
—Oil and gas	5,487	20,774	19,840	24,201	23,553	17,132	23,359	11,693	11,491	20,168	21,150
—Non-oil exports	635	582	592	518	523	543	812	645	340	284	357
Services exports	649	1,354	2,472	3,261	4,468	4,204	2,820	1,753	1,451	1,121	1,335
Merchandise imports	3,985	7,257	12,898	13,860	16,718	11,803	8,521	10,888	13,138	12,552	18,027
Services imports	2,629	3,153	5,280	6,443	8,885	9,957	6,487	5,621	3,590	3,288	4,457
Current account balance	154	12,267	4,707	7,660	2,816	104	11,968	-2,438	-3,446	5,733	358
Foreign exchange reserves	976	7,652	7,556	7,447	10,824	10,907	14,561	9,617	1,102	5,287	—
Gold reserves (*thousands of ounces*)	3,743	3,738	3,738	3,738	3,779	3,820	3,903	4,343	4,343	4,343	4,343
Exchange rate (*rials per U.S. $*)	68.88	67.63	67.64	70.22	70.62	70.48	70.48	70.62	78.33	83.6	86.36

1984–94

	1984	1985	1986	1987	1988	1989	1990	1991	1992	1993	1994
Merchandise exports	17,087	14,175	7,171	11,916	10,709	13,081	19,305	18,661	19,868	18,080	19,054
—Oil and gas	16,726	13,710	6,255	10,755	9,673	12,037	17,933	16,012	16,880	14,333	14,604
—Non-oil exports	361	465	916	1,161	1,036	1,044	1,312	2,649	2,988	3,747	4,450
Services exports	1,069	763	607	437	467	3,298	3,392	2,881	2,842	2,613	—
Merchandise imports	14,729	12,006	10,585	12,005	10,608	13,448	18,330	25,190	23,274	19,287	12,683
Services imports	3,841	3,408	2,348	2,437	2,437	3,122	4,040	5,800	5,940	5,743	—
Current account balance	-414	-476	-5,155	-2,090	-1,869	-191	-973	-10,248	-7,304	-4,515	4,581
Foreign exchange reserves	—	—	—	—	—	—	—	—	—	—	—
Gold reserves (*thousands of oz.*)	4,343	4,342	4,343	4,343	4,343	4,343	4,343	4,343	4,343	—	—
Exchange rate (*rials per U.S. $*)	90.03	91.05	78.76	71.46	68.68	72.02	68.1	67.51	65.55	1,267.77	1,748.75

Sources: International Monetary Fund, *International Financial Statistics*, various issues; Economist Intelligence Unit (EIU) *Country Report* and *Country Profile*, various issues. Notes: Natural gas exports are insignificant compared to oil exports. The most recent figures for foreign exchange reserves are from 1982. Since the 1980s, there have been multiple exchange rates; the figures for the "official" exchange rate are annual averages.

Table 6

IRANIAN NATIONAL ACCOUNTS
(in billions of current Iranian rials)

1973–83

	1973	1974	1975	1976	1977	1978	1979	1980	1981	1982	1983
Exports	642	1,478	1,440	1,787	1,751	1,189	1,762	883	945	1,864	1,885
Government consumption	313	639	818	1,004	1,134	1,245	1,223	1,380	1,676	1,910	2,151
Gross fixed capital formation (GFCF)	387	530	999	1,589	1,790	1,628	1,197	1,442	1,528	1,842	2,870
Changes in stocks	106	35	14	-251	-169	-479	99	520	295	-165	226
Private consumption	852	1,180	1,430	1,869	2,697	2,503	3,027	3,531	4,653	5,943	7,771
Imports	345	676	1,127	1,295	1,491	1,103	923	1,089	1,260	1,251	1,851
Gross domestic product (GDP)	1,764	3,090	3,512	4,697	5,948	5,179	5,970	6,632	8,009	10,540	13,376
Net factor income to/from abroad	-36	-11	-15	-5	-98	-186	56	26	33	—	-7
Gross national product (GNP)	1,728	3,079	3,497	4,692	5,850	4,993	6,025	6,658	8,042	10,540	13,370
GFCF (*as % of GDP*)—public sector	12.7	10.9	15.5	16.6	16.9	18.1	9.6	10.9	9.4	10.7	10
—private sector	9.2	6.3	12.9	17.2	13.2	13.3	10.5	10.8	9.6	6.8	11.5
—total	21.9	17.2	28.4	33.8	30.1	31.4	20.1	21.7	19.1	17.5	21.5
Public consumption (*as % of GDP*)	17.7	20.7	23.3	21.4	19.1	24	20.5	20.8	20.9	18.1	16.1
Private consumption (*as % of GDP*)	48.3	38.2	40.7	39.8	45.3	48.3	50.7	53.2	58.1	56.4	58.1
Total consumption (*as % of GDP*)	66	58.9	64	61.2	64.4	72.4	71.2	74	79	74.5	74.2

1984–94

	1984	1985	1986	1987	1988	1989	1990	1991	1992	1993	1994
Exports	1,570	1,251	553	837	1,514	2,773	8,058	9,596	11,545	22,240	39,097
Government consumption	2,190	2,443	2,371	2,707	3,199	3,294	4,054	5,367	6,927	13,644	19,798
Gross fixed capital formation (GFCF)	3,096	2,759	2,494	2,662	2,957	3,709	5,663	10,844	14,640	20,657	27,941
Changes in stocks	508	562	1,099	2,417	1,296	2,891	4,827	5,806	8,867	6,690	2,213
Private consumption	8,927	9,627	10,439	12,226	14,906	18,448	22,666	33,205	40,127	57,861	69,673
Imports	1,605	1,266	935	950	1,756	3,594	8,622	14,711	15,643	27,293	28,680
GDP	14,804	15,775	16,227	19,949	22,304	27,787	36,645	50,107	66,463	93,800	130,041
Net factor income to/from abroad	−11	−34	−19	−39	−116	−212	−339	−735	−823	−1,942	−3,517
GNP	14,793	15,742	16,208	19,910	22,188	27,575	36,305	49,372	65,640	91,858	126,525
GFCF (as % of GDP)—public sector	8.8	7	5.9	5.2	5.6	5.7	7.1	8.5	9	10.6	8.4
—private sector	12.1	10.5	9.5	8.1	7.7	7.6	8.3	13.2	13	11.4	13.1
—total	20.9	17.5	15.4	13.3	13.3	13.3	15.5	21.6	22	22	21.5
Public consumption (as % of GDP)	14.8	15.5	14.6	13.6	14.3	11.9	11.1	10.7	10.4	14.5	15.2
Private consumption (as % of GDP)	60.3	61.0	64.3	61.3	66.8	66.4	61.9	66.3	60.4	61.3	53.6
Total consumption (as % of GDP)	75.1	76.5	78.9	74.9	81.1	78.3	72.9	77	70.8	76.2	68.8

Sources: International Monetary Fund, *International Financial Statistics*, various issues; Central Bank of Iran, *Annual Report*, various issues. Notes: Exports and imports refer to goods and non-factor services. Gross fixed capital formation (GFCF) refers to gross investment excluding changes in stocks. Gross national product (GNP) equals gross domestic product (GDP) plus or minus net factor income. During this period and particularly in the 1980s, the difference between GNP and GDP was marginal.

Table 7

IRANIAN BUDGETS

1973–83

(in billions of Iranian rials)	1973	1974	1975	1976	1977	1978	1979	1980	1981	1982	1983
Revenues—taxes	131.2	157.8	270.8	342.9	443.6	465.9	368.3	349.4	554.1	613.9	796.5
—other	22.3	31.4	64.5	72	92.8	119.8	111.6	96.7	159.6	198.5	197.8
—oil and gas	311.3	1,205.2	1,246.8	1,421.4	1,497.8	1,013.2	1,219.7	888.8	1,056.4	1,689.5	1,729.4
—total	464.8	1,394.4	1,582.1	1,836.4	2,034.2	1,598.9	1,699.6	1,325.9	1,770.1	2,501.9	2,773.7
Expenditures—current	316.8	727.7	969.4	1,083.8	1,248.1	1,387.1	1,552	1,727.8	2,032.4	2,251.5	2,523.1
—capital	161.2	348.7	526.8	591.6	926.8	657.1	633.1	568.1	674.7	914.8	1,148.6
—total	478	1,254.4	1,775.9	2,006.2	2,492.2	2,207.8	2,227.9	2,298.4	2,707.1	3,167.4	3,672.3
—budget balance	-13.2	140	193.8	-169.8	-458	-608.9	-528.3	-972.5	-937	-665.5	-898.6
Budget balance (as % of GDP)	-0.7	4.5	-5.5	-3.6	-7.7	-11.8	-8.8	-14.7	-11.7	-6.3	-6.7
Capital expenditure (as % of GDP)	9.1	11.3	15	12.6	15.6	12.7	10.6	8.6	8.4	8.7	8.6
Oil and gas (as % of total)	67	86.4	78.8	77.7	73.6	63.4	71.8	67	59.7	67.5	62.3
GDP	1,764	3,090	3,512	4,897	5,948	5,179	5,970	6,632	8,009	10,540	13,376
Total expenditure (as % of GDP)	27.1	40.6	50.6	41	41.9	42.6	37.3	34.7	33.8	30.1	27.5

1984–94

	1984	1985	1986	1987	1988	1989	1990	1991	1992	1993	1994
Revenues—taxes	898.7	1,033.7	1,024.6	1,030.2	986.5	1,188	1,695	2,765	3,775.5	4,061.4	5,491
—other	442.9	443.9	266.1	375.1	431.1	1,215.9	2,819.7	3,129.6	5,040.6	6,281.1	—
—oil and gas	1,373.2	1,188.7	416.8	766.2	667.8	770.8	1,118.3	1,038.7	1,068.4	9,908.2	23,907
—total	2,714.8	2,666.3	1,707.5	2,171.5	2,085.4	3,174.7	5,633	6,933.3	9,884.5	20,250.7	—
Expenditures—current	2,475.6	2,517.6	2,338.6	2,900.3	3,387	3,381.2	4,475.5	5,561.4	7,779.4	13,777.6	—
—capital	878	765.2	746.5	729.2	816.5	931.5	1,766	2,527.1	2,949	6,425	9,586
—total	3,353.6	3,272.1	3,128.6	3,625.7	4,195.7	4,311	6,307.8	8,088.5	10,971.5	20,795.6	—
—budget bal.	-638.8	-605.8	-1,421.1	-1,454.2	-2,110.3	-1,136.3	-674.8	-1,155.2	-1,087	-544.9	—
Budget balance (% of GDP)	-4.3	-3.8	-8.8	-7.3	-9.5	-4.1	-1.8	-2.3	-1.6	-0.6	—
Capital expend. (% of GDP)	5.9	4.9	4.6	3.7	3.7	3.4	5	5	4.8	7.5	—
Oil and gas (% of total)	50.6	44.6	24.4	35.3	32	24.3	19.9	15	10.8	48.9	—
GDP	14,804	15,775	16,227	19,949	22,304	27,787	36,645	50,107	66,463	93,801	—
Total expend. (% of GDP)	22.7	20.7	19.3	18.2	18.8	15.5	17.2	16.1	16.5	22.2	—

Source: Central Bank of Iran, *Annual Report*, various issues. Notes: The Islamic year begins March 21. The *Annual Reports* note that the figures exclude "Special Revenues" and, presumably, off-budget military expenditures. Oil revenues are recorded in rials at the highly overvalued "official" exchange rate and thus the contribution of oil revenues to the budget (particularly in recent years) is grossly understated.

Table 8

IRANIAN LABOR AND LIVING STANDARDS

1974–84

	1974	1975	1976	1977	1978	1979	1980	1981	1982	1983	1984
Population (in millions)	32.5	33.4	33.7	34.7	36	37.9	39.6	41.2	42.8	44.4	46.2
Labor force (in millions)	9.25	9.45	9.79	10.6	10.32	10.61	10.89	11.36	11.75	12.10	12.46
Employed (in millions)	8.34	8.47	8.8	8.99	9.19	9.4	9.61	10	10.3	10.57	10.84
Unemployment rate (%)	9.9	10.3	9.2	10.5	10.9	11.4	11.7	12	12.3	12.6	13.1
% of population employed	25.7	25.4	26.1	25.9	25.5	24.8	24.3	24.3	24.1	23.8	23.5
Physicians	11,760	12,440	13,428	14,257	15,010	16,200	14,725	15,182	15,900	15,945	—
Population per physician	2,764	2,684	2,510	2,434	2,398	2,340	2,689	2,714	2,692	2,785	—
Hospital beds	44,279	49,194	49,870	55,217	56,830	55,688	59,152	59,152	59,500	64,117	—
Population per hospital bed	734	679	676	628	634	681	669	697	719	692	—
University students	135,354	151,904	154,215	160,308	175,625	174,217	—	—	117,148	121,048	145,809

1985–94

	1985	1986	1987	1988	1989	1990	1991	1992	1993	1994
Population (in millions)	47.8	49.4	51	51.9	53.2	54.5	55.8	57.2	58.5	59.8
Labor force (in millions)	12.64	12.82	13.24	13.62	13.99	14.77	15.35	—	—	—
Employed (in millions)	10.92	11	11.28	11.46	11.78	12.7	13.21	—	—	—
Unemployment rate (%)	13.6	14.1	14.8	15.9	15.8	14	13.9	11.4	11.2	8.7
% of population employed	22.8	22.3	22.1	22.1	22.1	23.3	23.7	—	—	—
Physicians	16,580	16,000	17,950	18,350	15,200	20,200	22,000	—	—	—
Population per physician	2,883	3,088	2,841	2,828	3,500	2,698	2,536	—	—	—
Hospital beds	66,587	67,000	73,500	81,000	82,085	82,694	85,810	—	—	—
Population per hospital bed	718	737	694	641	648	659	650	—	—	—
University students	151,495	167,971	204,862	250,709	—	312,076	344,045	375,579	—	—

Sources: Central Bank of Iran, *Economic Report and Balance Sheet*, various issues, and *Annual Review* (1993–94); Hisham Amirahmadi, *Revolution and Economic Transition: The Iranian Experience* (Albany, NY: State University of New York Press, 1990); Jahangir Amuzegar, *Iran's Economy under the Islamic Republic* (London: I. B. Taurus & Co., 1993). Notes: Unemployment rates are official estimates, which do not take into account "hidden" unemployment. The ratio of employed to total population takes account of both the labor force participation rate and the unemployment rate and is an indicator of the dependency ratio (the number of dependents per employed person). The gap in the report on health services in 1984 is not explained in official sources. Universities were closed for almost two years in 1980 and 1981. The report's omission of 1989 is not explained.

Table 9

IRAN'S INDUSTRIAL GDP BY SECTOR[9]

1974–83

(in billions of 1982–83 rials)	1974	1975	1976	1977	1978	1979	1980	1981	1982	1983
Agriculture	1,529	1,634	1,738	1,651	1,677	1,797	1,915	1,953	2,091	2,193
Oil (including refining)	5,514	4,886	5,508	5,211	3,784	2,847	870	883	1,958	2,022
Non-oil industry	901	1,049	1,204	1,036	900	799	1,108	1,203	1,174	1,302
Construction	515	743	1,062	941	818	763	763	671	696	937
GDP (factor cost)	9,492	9,735	11,120	11,568	9,886	9,487	7,512	7,454	8,838	10,051
Non-oil GDP	4,919	5,691	6,513	7,186	6,669	6,991	6,642	6,571	6,880	8,029
Non-oil goods	2,945	3,426	4,004	3,628	3,395	2,959	3,786	4,710	3,961	4,432
GDP-market (in constant 1990 prices)	39,735	40,847	48,326	51,995	41,040	37,227	32,036	31,249	35,336	40,012
Index of per capita GDP (1974=100)	100	100	117	122	93	81	66	62	68	74
Production index (large manufacturers)	55.7	63.9	74.9	83.8	71.8	72.2	77.1	88.1	100	121.9
—annual % change in production index	15	14.7	17.3	11.9	-14.3	0.5	6.3	14.3	13.5	21.9
Employment index (large manufacturers)	67.4	74.4	79	81.8	85.1	89.4	92.5	95.4	100	108.6
—annual % change in employment index	7.5	10.4	6.2	2.7	4.9	5.1	3.5	3.1	4.8	8.6

1984–94

	1984	1985	1986	1987	1988	1989	1990	1991	1992	1993	1994
Agriculture	2,354	2,538	2,651	2,716	2,648	2,746	2,968	3,120	3,352	3,536	3,690
Oil (including refining)	1,650	1,644	1,403	1,599	1,754	1,890	2,265	2,517	2,554	2,645	2,496
Non-oil industry	1,455	1,543	1,436	1,339	1,545	1,683	1,954	2,293	2,803	2,438	2,534
Construction	890	773	649	550	433	426	438	508	549	562	596
GDP (factor cost)	10,150	12,750	11,593	11,370	10,361	10,800	12,045	13,264	14,050	14,771	15,174
Non-oil GDP	8,500	11,106	10,190	9,771	8,607	8,910	9,781	10,747	11,496	12,127	12,678
Non-oil goods	4,699	4,859	4,736	4,605	4,626	4,855	5,359	5,921	6,284	6,536	6,820
GDP-market (constant 1990 prices)	40,378	40,494	34,360	34,760	31,742	32,793	36,645	40,354	42,816	43,806	44,576
GDP per capita index (1974=100)	71	69	57	56	50	50	55	59	61	61	61
Production index (large manu.)	131.3	126.9	100.6	94.2	86.7	91.8	118.7	141.3	143.2	129.3	—
—annual % change	7.7	3.4	-20.7	-6.4	-8	5.9	29.3	19	1.3	-9.7	—
Employment index (large manu.)	115.3	118.5	114	110.8	111.1	111.2	114.7	120.8	120.6	114.8	—
—annual % change	6.2	2.8	-3.8	-2.8	0.3	0.1	3.1	5.3	-0.2	-4.8	—

Sources: Central Bank of Iran, *Annual Report*, various issues; International Monetary Fund, *International Financial Statistics*, various issues. Notes: Non-oil industry includes manufacturing, mining, electric power, and water. Non-oil goods sector refers to non-oil GDP excluding services. It includes agriculture, industry, and construction. Large manufacturing establishments are those with ten or more employees.

Table 10

IRAN'S NATIONAL ACCOUNTS IN CONSTANT PRICES[10]

1974–1983

	1974	1975	1976	1977	1978	1979	1980	1981	1982	1983
Exports	5,117	4,594	5,120	4,660	3,171	2,742	869	843	1,726	1,899
Government consumption	2,123	2,461	2,887	2,830	2,695	2,154	1,968	1,948	1,910	1,930
Investment	1,843	2,869	3,872	3,551	3,043	1,889	1,843	1,724	1,842	2,551
—Private	738	1,362	2,088	1,546	1,306	922	879	815	690	1,315
—Public	1,105	1,507	1,784	2,005	1,737	967	964	909	1,152	1,236
Change in stocks	83	31	-492	-511	-727	127	727	338	-165	159
Private consumption	4,287	4,879	5,717	6,191	6,415	5,610	5,360	5,533	5,943	6,804
Imports	1,337	1,990	2,253	2,475	1,680	1,207	1,175	1,290	1,251	1,883
GDP	12,083	12,183	14,415	14,822	12,889	11,773	9,556	9,321	10,540	11,935

1984–1994

	1984	1985	1986	1987	1988	1989	1990	1991	1992	1993	1994
Exports	1,546	1,400	1,221	1,557	1,730	1,866	2,253	2,529	2,718	3,155	3,101
Government consumption	1,811	1,896	1,508	1,403	1,396	1,189	1,337	1,450	1,552	1,820	1,953
Investment	2,562	2,153	1,646	1,361	1,144	1,217	1,379	1,943	2,077	2,133	2,205
—Private	1,401	1,212	916	822	663	692	766	1,136	1,143	1,244	1,564
—Public	1,161	941	730	539	480	525	613	807	934	890	641
Change in stocks	318	286	411	698	288	549	822	821	1,010	111	579
Private consumption	7,170	7,291	6,544	6,141	6,172	6,327	7,794	8,528	8,721	8,927	9,200
Imports	1,638	1,305	946	1,006	791	986	1,274	1,651	1,627	1,362	835
GDP	12,044	12,072	10,249	10,368	10,594	11,067	12,310	13,620	14,451	15,072	15,045

Sources: International Monetary Fund, *International Financial Statistics*; Central Bank of Iran, *Annual Report*, various issues; and UN, *National Accounts Statistics*, 1992 and earlier issues. Notes: Figures are in billions of 1982–83 Iranian rials. Export and import figures are for goods and non-factor services. GDP figures are adjusted for terms of trade and statistical discrepancies not shown in the table.

Table 11

IRANIAN AGRICULTURE[11]

1974–83

	1974	1975	1976	1977	1978	1979	1980	1981	1982	1983
Agricultural production index (1979–81=100)	83.6	85.7	95	93.2	97.8	94.8	96.1	109.2	119.5	119.1
Agricultural production index *per capita*	100.8	100.3	108.8	103.6	105.4	98.7	96.3	105	109.8	104.5
Exports *(in millions of U.S. $)*	239	301	276	326	314	305	142	118	137	157
Imports *(in millions of U.S. $)*	1,274	2,018	1,485	1,943	1,445	1,855	2,171	2,775	2,491	2,816
Agriculture trade balance *(in millions of U.S. $)*	−1,035	−1,717	−1,209	−1,617	−1,131	−1,550	−2,029	−2,657	−2,354	−2,659
% of labor force in agriculture	40.6	39.9	39.2	38.5	37.9	37.2	36.4	35.5	34.5	33.5

1984–93

	1984	1985	1986	1987	1988	1989	1990	1991	1992	1993
Agricultural production index (1979–81=100)	125.3	134.8	147.8	149.1	146	146.7	168.2	182.1	191.4	198.9
Agricultural production index *per capita*	105.2	108.5	114.3	111.2	105.1	101.8	113.6	119.6	122.4	123.9
Exports *(in millions of U.S. $)*	177	228	394	449	394	482	447	546	633	—
Imports *(in millions of U.S. $)*	2,689	2,090	1,462	1,678	1,587	3,178	2,673	2,488	2,445	—
Agriculture trade balance *(in millions of U.S. $)*	−2,512	−1,862	−1,068	−1,229	−1,193	−2,697	−2,226	−1,942	−1,812	—
% of labor force in agriculture	32.4	31.5	30.6	29.8	29.1	—	—	—	27.7	—

Sources: U.S. Department of Agriculture, various reports; Central Bank of Iran, *Annual Reports*.

Table 12

SUMMARY OF IRAN'S AVERAGE ANNUAL GROWTH RATES[12]

	1970–77	1977–80	1980–85	1985–88	1988–91	1992	1993	1994	1977–94
Oil production	5.5	–35.7	11	0.5	9.6	9.7	–2.8	0	–35.5
Agricultural production	4.6	1	7	2.7	7.6	5.1	4	—	113.5
Non-oil industry—value added	11.4	2.3	6.9	0	14.1	22.2	–13	3.9	144.6
Index of production—manufacturing	15.7	–2.7	10.5	–12	17.7	1.3	–9.7	—	54.3
Gross domestic product (GDP)	10.6	–15	4.8	–7.7	8.3	6.1	2.3	1.8	–14.3
GDP *per capita*	7.6	18.5	1	–11.1	5.7	3.5	0	–0.9	–50.5
Non-oil GDP	12.6	–13.5	8.1	–8.2	7.7	7	5.5	4.5	76.4
Non-oil GDP *per capita*	9.5	–16.8	4.1	–10.8	5.1	4.4	3.1	2.3	2.4
Living standards	10.7	–8	1.5	–10	11.4	–5.1	14.7	–12.8	19.6
Gross fixed capital formation	21	–19.5	3.2	–19	19.3	6.8	2.7	3.4	–37.9

Sources: The data are derived from the previous tables. Estimates for 1970–73/74 are from the Central Bank of Iran, *Annual Report*, various issues. Figures for agricultural production are from the U.S. Department of Agriculture. GDP estimates are from International Monetary Fund, *International Financial Statistics* (various issues) in constant 1990 prices. Notes: The choice of terminal years for the various periods is based on important events and/or changes. The column labeled "1977–94" compares 1994 to 1977, the peak year of economic performance under the shah; for manufacturing, this column refers to 1977–93. Non-oil industry refers to value added in manufacturing and mining as well as electricity and water. The index of manufacturing is based on production by establishments employing ten or more people. Living standards are measured by changes in real private consumption *per capita*, calculated from national accounts. Gross fixed capital formation refers to investment (excluding changes in stocks).

THE WASHINGTON INSTITUTE POLICY PAPERS SERIES

THE WASHINGTON INSTITUTE POLICY FOCUS SERIES

RECENT PUBLICATIONS OF THE WASHINGTON INSTITUTE

Building for Security and Peace in the Middle East: An American Agenda— a comprehensive blueprint for U.S. Middle East policy during the second Clinton administration from the Institute's bipartisan Presidential Study Group.

Making Peace with the PLO: The Rabin Government's Road to the Oslo Accord—A detailed assessment by *Ha'aretz* correspondent David Makovsky of the personal, domestic, and international factors that led Yitzhak Rabin and Israel's Labor government to conduct secret peace negotiations in Oslo with the-Palestinians.

Supporting Peace: America's Role in an Israel-Syria Peace Agreement—A study of the role that U.S. forces could play in monitoring and maintaining an Israel-Syria peace agreement, by Michael Eisenstadt, Andrew Bacevich, and Carl Ford.

Approaching Peace: American Interests in Israeli-Palestinian Final Status Talks—A collection of essays presenting specific policy recommendations for Washington's role in reaching a final peace agreement. The contributors are Samuel Lewis, Hermann Eilts, Richard Haass, Peter Rodman, Eugene Rostow, William Quandt, Harvey Sicherman, and Kenneth Stein.

Peacewatch: The Arab-Israeli Peace Process and U.S. Policy—A comprehensive analytical and documentary record of the Arab-Israeli peace process from January 1993 to March 1994, by the staff and associates of the Washington Institute.

Democracy in the Middle East: Defining the Challenge—A series of essays on U.S. efforts to promote democracy in the Middle East, by Graham Fuller, Mohammed Abdelbeki Hermassi, Martin Kramer, Joshua Muravchik, and Laurie Mylroie.

UN Security Council Resolution 242: The Building Block of Peacemaking—A collection of papers examining the resolution's history and relevance for current Arab-Israeli negotiations, featuring Adnan Abu Odeh, Nabil Elaraby, Meir Rosenne, Eugene Rostow, Dennis Ross, and Vernon Turner.

Democracy and Arab Political Culture—An examination by the late historian Elie Kedourie of the political traditions of Islam and the introduction of Western ideas into the Middle East in the nineteenth century.

The Politics of Change in the Middle East—A collection of essays by distinguished Middle East scholars examining regional political stability and regime succession.

For a complete catalogue of publications, contact:

The Washington Institute *for Near East Policy*
1828 L Street NW, Suite 1050
Washington, DC 20036
Phone (202) 452-0650 • Fax (202) 223-5364
E-mail: info@washingtoninstitute.org
Internet: www.washingtoninstitute.org